Music Education

MUSIC
EDUCATION

Psychology and Method

ERIK FRANKLIN

GEORGE G. HARRAP & CO. LTD

London   Toronto   Wellington   Sydney

First published in Great Britain 1972
by GEORGE G. HARRAP & CO. LTD
182–184 High Holborn, London WC1V 7AX

ISBN 0 245 50659 4

Set in 10/12pt. Monotype Plantin, printed by letterpress,
and bound in Great Britain at The Pitman Press, Bath

Preface

One of the fundamental difficulties in the training of music teachers has been to integrate the knowledge achieved in general psychology, music psychology, general method, and music method. The students are usually advised to read different books in the four fields and are then supposed to find the connections themselves between the different subjects.

It has been my aim in the present book to help the student teacher —whether he intends to become a music-teacher, a teacher in a particular instrument, or a class teacher with music as one of his subjects— to find this integration. In order to make it possible all these different subjects have been dealt with, as much as possible, in connection with music or music teaching. Let me give just one illustration: a child's animism during its first school years belongs to the field of general developmental *psychology*, but examples of animistic music teaching, in the chapter on development in this book, are examples of *method*.

It has been my dilemma to decide what to include and what to exclude. Although the subject matter is overwhelming I decided to restrict the content to a brief survey. One of the reasons is that psychology and method in several music-teacher schools are rather secondary subjects. Most of the students' time is devoted to the practice of skills in voice and instruments. In schools such as these a small book suits the curriculum, while an extensive handbook would be totally neglected. Those who have more time to spend will still have the benefit of a concentrated introduction, before going on to the specialized literature.

Being a Swede it has often been difficult for me to find the correct expressions in English. I would have preferred an Englishman to do the translation, had I found one familiar not only with the language but also with the terminology both in music and psychology. However, I want to express my thanks to Dr Arnold Bentley of Reading University, who has made a careful scrutiny of the language. If the language is still not idiomatic, it is because he did not want to change the content or rewrite the whole book, and therefore I hope the reader will forgive either myself or Dr Bentley.

Erik Franklin

Gothenburg
January 1971

Contents

The Psychological Fields of Research

1

When the concept of psychology was created it meant literally the science of the soul (*psyche* = soul or mind, *logos* = science). Nowadays however, we are not always able to distinguish between what concerns the body and what belongs to the mind. If a piano student before his debut or an examination gets a stomach-ache or even a gastric ulcer, because of nervousness about his performances, these stomach troubles have not only a physical but also a mental cause. It is obvious, therefore, that we need a new definition of psychology and it is generally agreed that the *science of experience and behaviour* is more apt.

In psychology there are many different fields of research: educational psychology, medical psychology, social psychology, differential psychology, psychology of perception, psychology of motivation, developmental psychology, psychology of emotions, etc. Even if specialists carry on research within their respective fields, it is a mistake to regard these fields as being isolated from each other. On the contrary, it is often the case that results from various fields contribute to the solution of an important and common psychological problem. Thus the boundaries between the different fields remain very vague. The unhappy piano student mentioned above is first of all a case for *educational psychology*, as a problem in respect of learning, but the causes of his stomach-ache come under *medical psychology*. On a different occasion, a piano student's nervousness may be due to the fact that he compares himself with his cleverer friends. In that case we look for explanations within *social psychology*, i.e., the psychology of group behaviour. How do group members behave within their group? How does a certain group behave in comparison with other groups?

A piano student may fail for lack of talent—then *differential psychology* provides the material for an investigation. Differential psychology deals particularly with differences of talent and achievement and the measurement of these. The student may have difficulty in reading music scores —then he is a case for *psychology of perception*. It must be remembered, incidentally, that we do not only perceive with our eyes. All our different sense-organs supply impressions, which contribute to our perception and, therefore, hearing belongs essentially to perceptional psychology too.

Psychology of motivation teaches us that our motives govern our behaviour. When we are hungry, we are governed by our need for food and make efforts to procure some. When our merits are acknowledged by other people our need for self-confidence is fulfilled. Perhaps it was the approval of the teacher that our student needed. He lost his self-reliance and failed. *Developmental psychology* covers the development of man's behaviour from the prenatal stage (before birth) up to maturity. Perhaps a student has puberty problems, which makes him not only nervous of performing but also generally inhibited. We can also take it for granted that a student who fails feels unhappy and disappointed. The effects of these feelings on his behaviour lie within the scope of *emotional psychology*.

Psychology of music naturally deals primarily with psychological problems related to music. But as we have seen when trying to grasp the piano student's problems the borders between the different fields are very indistinct. The psychology of music must use the experience of the other psychological fields of research to solve problems within its own field. Similarly other fields of research should utilize the results of research obtained within music psychology. In particular a profitable exchange should be possible between differential psychology and psychology of perception on the one side and psychology of music on the other side.

Perception

2

Our knowledge of the outer world is communicated to us by our senses: sight, hearing, taste, smell, etc. The stimuli to which our ears react consist of wave movements which are brought to the brain and transformed into—perceived as—sounds. As a physical reality the wave movement is something that can be objectively measured so we should have here a good foundation in the psychology of perception. In the following chapters about the musical ear and differential psychology we will deal among other things with tests of musical talent which have been constructed on the basis of this objective background.

The discussion in this chapter about Weber's law is also based on that approach, which is called *psycho-physical*, because it deals with *psychological experience as having a physical cause*. The rest of the chapter, however, is devoted to the final psychological experience of perception, irrespective of psycho-physics. Although this experience is necessarily subjective there is still a pattern to be found.

Weber's law

Suppose that we have the possibility of working with a number of organ pipes exactly alike which consequently—when sounded one at a time—give the same pitch with exactly the same loudness. If we start by making one single organ pipe sound and then turn on another pipe we perceive a certain difference in loudness between the note of the single pipe and that of the two simultaneous pipes. The reinforced two-pipe note is, however, not twice as loud as the note of one pipe, which we might expect. If—with two pipes sounding—we turn on still one more pipe, so that we are listening to three simultaneous pipes, we again perceive an increase in loudness. But this third pipe does not add as much in loudness as the second did. A fourth pipe makes a hardly—if at all—noticeable difference. The addition of a fifth pipe is definitely not noticeable. Instead we must now add two pipes to the four, i.e., also a sixth, to notice any difference at all.

What we have come across here is Weber's law, dating from 1834. It is expressed mathematically by the formula

$$\frac{\Delta s}{s} = W$$

where Δs^1 denotes the least noticeable addition in stimulus, s the original stimulus, and W, called the Weber Fraction, is a constant. The constant W varies according to different senses. For loudness[2] it is about $\frac{1}{3}$. The law has been revised by the psychologist Fechner, and is therefore sometimes called the Weber-Fechner law. Even if it later turned out to be inexact, the general outlook is still valid. The discussions about the Weber law and its Fechner version have given rise to the term decibel as a standard measure of loudness. We shall have reason to return to this in a subsequent section.

The musical applicability of the law is clear. If there are nine violinists in the first violin-part of a symphony orchestra, it is useless to add just one violinist if you want an increase of loudness. According to Weber's law we get

$$\frac{\Delta s}{s} = \frac{1}{9}$$

$\frac{1}{9}$ is, however, too low as W must be at least $\frac{1}{3}$. Thus the law shows us that we must add at least three violinists to obtain a noticeable increase of loudness. With an addition of three violinists, we get

$$\frac{\Delta s}{s} = \frac{3}{9} = \frac{1}{3}$$

Of course, Weber's law also applies to speech and singing. For example, a singer can easily produce the very small change required in physical energy (the tension of the vocal cords) in order to produce a hardly noticeable difference in loudness, when singing on the level of pp. To produce a hardly noticeable difference in loudness on the level of ff requires a much greater physical effort. This is quite in accordance with the experience of several choir conductors who claim that it is rather difficult to bring about dynamic gradations between mf and ff in a choir. Public speakers should bear in mind that subtle variations brought about by small differences of physical energy are often the most effective.

Selectivity

Among the multitude of sensations that pour in through our sense-organs, only a few are consciously registered in our perception. We

---

[1] Δ, Greek letter, pronounced delta.
[2] Some scientists use the word intensity as a synonym for loudness. In psycho-physics, one should distinguish between intensity as a property of the stimulus, and loudness as the brain's interpretation, i.e., perception, of the intensity of the stimulus. Thus, when adding a second pipe to a single one, the intensity of the stimulus is doubled, but the brain does not perceive the doubled stimulus as a doubled loudness.

make a selection, attend to that which is more or less unconsciously governed by our needs, interests, appreciations, and attitudes. We can express it simply: we see what we want to see and hear what we want to hear.

If a group of tourists passes a music-shop, one of them will perhaps stop in front of it. He is interested in music. The others have not 'seen' the shop window. A bit further ahead some of them stop to look at the menu outside a restaurant. They stopped because they felt hungry. Their non-hungry friends did not 'see' the restaurant. Our perception is controlled by our interests and needs. This subjectivity reappears in most of our observations of the surrounding world and thus concerns also our hearing, and our experience of music. According to our attitudes, appreciations, needs, and interests, we approve of certain kinds of music whereas we disapprove of others. As teachers of music we should consider what kind of music our pupils are likely to approve of and how we must present 'our' music to make them select and attend to it as 'theirs'.

The perception of form and principles of grouping

However, not only our interests and needs make perception subjective. Perception is also in itself subjective. We cannot, for instance, be sure that our perception of relative proportions is exact. Consider as an example the two lines shown in figure 1. Placed beside each other they seem to be of the same length. Placed perpendicularly to each other they seem to be of different lengths. If you measure them with a ruler, or any other objective measure, you will see how far you can trust your eyes. Observations like this have made it clear that a psychological entity, a 'whole', is experienced as something more than the sum of its elements. The inversion is also true. The elements are experienced differently depending upon the wholeness to which they belong.

In music transposition is an illustration of the validity of the law. A tune can be regarded as the sum of a number of pitches. If you raise the pitch of all the notes of a melody, so that it is in the key of D major instead of the original C major, you will have a sum of pitches which is different from the original sum, but the melody will be recognized as the original tune.[1]

It can easily be demonstrated that the inversion of the law is valid. The notes C and G in a C major tune constitute the tonic and the

[1] An instance of visual transposition is the enlargement or reduction of a photograph.

13

dominant respectively, with the characteristics of these positions in the scale. If the same notes are used in a G major tune, however, the note C becomes a subdominant and G gets the function of a tonic.

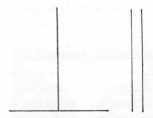

Fig. 1. Are the two lines of different length?

Another example is the displacement of the bar-lines as shown in Fig. 2. The notes and the measures and the sums of the notes and measures are the same, but the detail of the bar lines is changed and thus the musical meaning as a whole.

Fig. 2. The first subject in Haydn's *Symphony No. 94 in G major*, second movement. The original theme is above. Below the theme has been changed by moving the bar lines one quaver to the right.

The perception of melodies as structural entities, as musical form, have brought us into the field of form perception. In addition to the main principle of form perception cited above, psychology recognizes a number of form-creating factors or principles of grouping, which have chiefly been investigated in the visual field but which also, though not always, can be applied to hearing. We shall subsequently see illustrations of both visual and auditory applications.

Figure-ground-relation

The distinction between figure and ground and the law of wholeness is, like Weber's law, of a fundamental nature, and is to a certain extent the basis of the following principles of grouping. It signifies that we perceive figures, structures, and contours against a neutral background.

At the same time it signifies that we have difficulty in perceiving simultaneously two objects with partly the same contours. Either of the two observed objects becomes figure and the other background. The significance of this law of perception is made clear by Fig. 3. You see either a white vase or two black faces in profile. The vase and the profiles alternate.

Fig. 3. Rubin's vase figure.

The utilization of the figure-ground-relation is of auditory value. Primarily it provides a clear picture of the meaning of rhythm and time (pulse), rhythm being figure, and time the ground, in a figure-ground-relation. This definition is no doubt superior to other current definitions of rhythm and time.

It is obvious that a melody against the background of accompaniment constitutes a figure-ground-relation. A problem falling under this category is that of teaching piano students how to play two notes against three. There is usually a melody of two-note groups of quavers in the treble and accompanying triplets in a figural bass. The execution should be regarded with respect to the definition of rhythm-time above. The triplets should in other words be looked upon as an indistinct background, both as to pitch and time, to the distinctly contoured treble melody. The first note of the two figures played simultaneously in treble and bass respectively constitute a simultaneous time-experienced contour. What happens musically is thus, in this case, somewhat similar to the visual instance of Rubin's vase (see Fig. 3). After looking at the problem from this angle we realize that it must be extremely difficult to pay quite the same amount of attention to bass and treble. Either one or the other emerges. But it is the intention that one should emerge and not the other.

A way of learning the technique is to practise the bass movement until that can be played more or less automatically. Then the melody movement with its possibilities of expression is added while the bass continues to go on as a vague background. Another way, of course, is to make the pupil count the bass triplets *"one* and two *and* three and"* with the treble notes on the spaced out syllables. That will form a mechanically correct technique in a slow tempo to start with. Sooner or later, however, the figure-ground-relation will have to emerge as an artistic claim and of necessity in a faster movement.

The factor of proximity

The factor of proximity states that our conception of structures is determined by the proximity between the observed elements, a statement in itself quite simple. Fig. 4 gives a visual illustration, Fig. 5 a musical one.

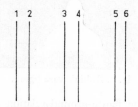

Fig. 4. On account of the factor of proximity, we perceive the lines 1—2, 3—4, and 5—6 as pairs. It is more difficult to perceive the lines 2—3 or 4—5 as pairs.

Fig. 5. The factor of proximity makes it easier to experience alternative (*a*) than alternative (*b*) as a melody.

The factor of similarity

The effect of the factor of similarity on our perception of structure is made clear by Fig. 6 (*a*). The factors of similarity and proximity often compete for dominance in the form structure.

The significance of the chronological course

The factor of similarity brings up the question about the auditory form perception as compared to the visual form perception. The visual laws

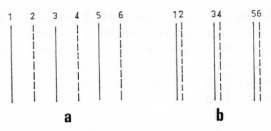

Fig. 6 (*a*). The factor of similarity makes you group together 1—3—5, and 2—4—6. To match 1 and 2, 3 and 4, 5 and 6, respectively is not so easily done as in Fig. 4. However, there exists a certain rivalry. In Fig. 6 (*b*) the continuous and the dotted lines have been drawn more closely together, with the result that the factor of proximity definitely prevails.

of perception need not necessarily have auditory correspondence. The auditory perception always has a chronological course which is lacking in the visual form perception. Owing to the significance of the chronological course the immediate memory span plays an important part. It is improbable that the factor of similarity can be directly transferred to the field of music. Who would suggest that a series of notes of equal length and pitch would be interpreted more easily as a melody than a series of dissimilar notes? Even if a sequence of exactly similar notes were to be experienced as belonging together, they could not in any way be regarded as more structural than other series of notes. We will return to the question of particularly auditory-musical factors of form perception.

The factor of good figure

The factor of good figure demonstrates that "psychological organization is always as good as existing circumstances admit" (Koffka). A good, distinct figure is more easily remembered than one that is not distinct (Fig. 7).

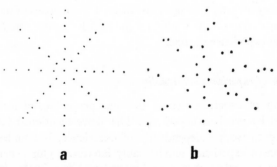

Fig. 7 (*a*) is a distinct, (*b*) a non-distinct, figure. The number of dots is equal in both structures, but (*b*) is considerably more difficult to recollect.

Perhaps composers of popular songs could tell us what gives a melody a good figure? We can, however, establish that the factor of good figure affects our perception of melody, though a melody is considerably more complicated and has more dimensions than the visual structures in Fig. 7. Present, and eventually latent, harmony has a certain influence as well as time and rhythm.

The factor of closeness

The factor of closeness concerns the perception of closed surfaces and figures. The individual lines are not experienced as isolated, but as parts forming together a delimited unity. As usual, however, there may occur rivalry between various factors of form perception to the effect that what is two-dimensional may withdraw in favour of a one-dimensional good figure (Fig. 8).

a   b

Fig. 8. The factor of closeness shows in (a) three delimited figures. In (b) the three delimited figures have been put together, so that the curved main line, the factor of good figure, successfully competes with the factor of closeness.

The factors of closeness and good figure co-operating can also be seen as an instance of figure-ground-relation. The musical application of this law we have seen earlier (see page 15).

A musical application of a simple factor of closeness concerning delimited surfaces of music or figures may be possible, but drawing too far-reaching parallels between visual and auditory perception can result in absurdity. All music is in itself multi-dimensional in that the experiences of time and pitch co-operate. Comparisons between visual and auditory art would be more adequate, if the mobiles of modern art were compared to music. Within art the mobiles indicate an attempt to express an experience of time.

The factor of experience and tonality

The factor of experience states that our perception of structure is influenced by previous experience. The above-mentioned factors are considered to work independently of experience, but under certain circumstances experience unmistakably interferes. Our experience of letters has the effect that even incomplete letters make sense (see Fig. 9).

In tonal music, perception of tonality can be looked upon as a perceptive factor of experience. It is tempting to consider the perception of tonality also to be a factor of closeness. The complete cadence of tonic-subdominant-dominant-tonic thus could be considered a delimited triangle. It is probably wise, however, in this case as in many

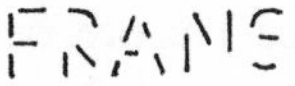

FRANS

Fig. 9. Because of previous experience we have no difficulty in interpreting the incomplete letters as the name FRANS.

others, not to make comparisons with the visual field too categorical. The perception of tonality is a typically musical experience with many dimensions, not forgetting the time factor that goes together with the harmonic progressions. Fig. 10 shows an example of the experience of tonality.

Fig. 10. The example has been borrowed from Franklin's tonality test. The person giving the test plays the melody but leaves out the last note (the keynote), which the subject has to fill in himself (singing some syllable, humming, or whistling).

Attempts have been made by musicologists to enlarge the concept of tonality in order to make it fit modern styles of music. This is quite confusing as outstanding contemporary composers of these same styles spare no effort in pointing out that their music is atonal. In the author's opinion the concept of tonality should be maintained in its present very clear and limited sense. For new experiences new terminology should be created, e.g., the concept of musical *focus* instead of tonic for an atonal central tone or other structural centrum. The psychological experience of this musical focus might as well be called *focusness*. Anyhow serious attempts ought to be made to create new terms instead of distorting the sense of an established concept.

Repetition and contrast

In addition to the general principles of grouping mentioned above, which have proved applicable to the perception of music, we must discuss the formative principles of *repetition* and *contrast*, well-known from the theory of composition. Here it is not a question of the grouping of simultaneous elements as with the visually applied laws, but of a form perception of a wider scope, where memory plays an important part. You like to hear what you recognize, i.e., the principle of repetition. You grow tired of the recognized and want something else, i.e., the principle of contrast. Music abounds in instances where composers in various ways have created balance between these two perceptive principles. Partly they did so in order to make their works appear homogeneous by the repetition of thematic contents, partly in order to avoid monotony by introducing a contrasting theme or some other element of contrast. An illustrative example is the simple *a-b-a* form, used in many tunes, where *a* denotes repeated contents, *b* the contrast. The recurring *a*-part in bigger forms, a march for instance, is often denoted by *da capo al fine*. (See other examples of musical form in Chapter 10.)

Atonality—some viewpoints

It is hardly probable that any kind of music could remain completely independent of the above-mentioned form-factors and principles. Many composers seem so anxious for originality, that they refrain from using repetition to the extent that the listener requires. This is especially the case with twelve-note music. In tonal music the listener profits from the repetition inherent in the system with its cadences, etc. Even a visually comparative form perception of a major scale and chromatic scale shows us on one side the structure of a major scale with fixed groups of whole and half tone steps, whereas the chromatic scale lacks such groups and points of support (see Fig. 11).

Fig. 11. The circles of the lower line show a visual grouping of the whole and half steps of the major scale. In the upper line there are the steps of the chromatic scale, which contains only half steps.

Tonality thus contains in itself a musical customary repetition, which helps the listener to perceive the musical form. In atonal serial music the composer must, for each new musical work, give the listener a new 'pattern' for listening, which the listener needs time to get acquainted with. If the composer does not pay sufficient attention to the principle of repetition, the listener who thinks that the piece is falling apart may be forgiven. To this principle of repetition must be added the importance of the immediate memory span. You cannot remember an unlimited number of different successive elements. You discover this easily if you try to repeat a number of arbitrary figures, or a series of atonally arranged notes. The immediate memory span is used as a measurement of tone memory in tests of musical talent (see Chapter 5). Very few people are able to reproduce an atonal series of twelve different notes after listening to it only once. A solution to this problem would be to compose shorter series, with fewer than twelve notes, which some composers of atonal music have tried.

Fig. 12. Below: Beethoven's *Symphony No. 5*, the opening motive. Above: a twelve-note series from Bela Bartok's *Violin Concerto* (bars 79–81). Notice how a genius instinctively uses the principle of repetition in the form of a rising fourth. The effects of syncopation and the grouping made by the slurs (bowing) are also worth attention.

When using series, 'themes', of as many as twelve notes, you must pay attention to the principle of repetition to a greater extent than when using a short motive of, say, four notes, as in Beethoven's *5th Symphony*.

The figure-ground-relation can be made to disappear through camouflage. The letter c can be concealed if it is reversed and made part of a bigger form, e.g., the figure 5. The protective colours of animals save them from discovery. A composer can completely destroy the significance (good figure) of a twelve-note series by mixing different series simultaneously in a polyphonic pattern. A mirror-image, or reversed presentation, of a series is from the listener's point of view meaningless if the series has not first been impressed by clear rhythm and distinct pitch-progressions in surroundings which do not serve as camouflage.

Our pupils will benefit by these viewpoints, if we

1. repeat a series several times, before we expect the pupils to appreciate it.

2. notice occurring repetitions within the actual series as to rhythms or intervals (see Fig. 12).

3. point out what makes the series stand out as a good figure and reduces camouflage. Bowing, phrasing, syncopation and dynamics are of interest in this connection (see Fig. 12).

4. to begin with choose short pieces or songs with series shorter than twelve notes, or series on the border between tonality and atonality (See page 108, point 4).

5. avoid camouflage in our own arrangements of atonal instrumental or vocal music. Short songs may be text-notated (see page 97).

Attention

We have seen how our perception is influenced by Weber's law, by our attitudes and motives, and how the form-perceptive factors and principles work. We shall now see how the concentrated form of perception, which we call attention, is affected by exterior and interior factors, both of which we will call attention factors.

The exterior factors are size, intensity, change and movement, and repetition. The interior factors are needs, interests, appreciations, and attitudes. Attention plays an important part in commercial advertising, but is of equal importance to teachers, who must try to 'sell' knowledge and proficiency.

The size factor

The size factor is utilized in advertising, e.g., in shop windows. A big sign sells more than a small sign. A teacher varies the size of his handwriting and sketches on the blackboard according to what he wants his pupils to memorize.

The intensity factor

The teacher utilizes the intensity factor in his voice. A loud voice tends to draw more attention to itself than a soft voice, but in teaching should only be used when absolutely necessary (see next paragraph).

Change and movement

One attention factor seldom works in isolation. The factors of size and intensity already mentioned lose their importance if they are not combined with the factor of change and movement. A sign which is alternately switched on and off attracts more attention than one that is on all the time. A voice continuously perceived as loud grows monotonous and tiring if it is not changed. Thus a teacher should vary the intensity of his voice as everything else that concerns his way of teaching.

The factor of repetition

Advertising and propaganda cannot afford to disregard any of the factors of attention, least of all the factor of repetition. Repetition is just as important and indispensable to the teacher. Repeated facts attract more attention and are also better remembered than those not recapitulated. Here as elsewhere, however, it is important that different factors are combined. Monotony of repetition should be avoided by variety of methods and by giving different motives for repetition.

The needs

Among the interior factors of attention our needs are of special importance. These needs govern not only our attention but to a great extent our actions as a whole. The needs are both biological and social.

Biological needs

Biological needs are congenital. To this category belong the needs for food and water, the sexual need, the need for oxygen, for rest and sleep, etc. These biological needs naturally influence our behaviour and they must be satisfied. At school they influence the timetable. The breaks for lunch and recreation at school are not waste of time but necessary interruptions to satisfy the needs for food, oxygen, and bodily movement. A hungry pupil is an inattentive pupil. At the same time the need to earn a living in the long term is, for older students, a good motive for assiduous studies. In the short term, however, the biological needs are of a kind that distract the pupil from his school-work.

Social needs

Social needs are acquired. They concern our relationships with our fellow beings. We need a sense of community, success and approval, economic security, emotional confidence, and self-esteem. New experiences, the realization of the self according to one's qualifications, are other social needs. We experience all these needs together with, or in comparison with, our fellow beings. When the teacher praises or blames his pupil, he exploits his pupil's social needs for confidence and approval. A pupil who is blamed feels insecure. The pupil who is praised experiences security and his need for approval is satisfied. The cribber may have an underdeveloped need for self-respect, which the teacher should try to reinforce. The fact that these needs are not congenital enables teachers, parents and all who are involved in the education of young people to sharpen their attention in a pedagogic situation and to educate personalities while teaching.

Obstacles to the satisfaction of our needs create various kinds of conflicts. Here the teacher must keep his eyes open. A pupil who never gains approval loses interest and enters into a latent conflict with his teacher. In the end the pupil may even run away from the conflict situation and shirk school. If he takes private music lessons, he may turn to another teacher instead or stop playing altogether. Of course criticism is a legitimate way of attracting the attention of the pupil and improving his learning, but to criticism should be added an expression of the teacher's belief in his pupil.

The halo effect

The remaining interior factors of attention, i.e., interest, appreciation, and attitudes, are intimately connected with each other. To a great extent it is a matter of the so called 'halo effect'. The expression 'halo effect'—originally an astronomical term—is used to denote a significant error, which is quite common when we form an opinion of a person. It shows itself when our opinion of a person in a certain known respect is unconsciously allowed to influence our opinion of the same person in other respects of which we are truly ignorant.

Pedagogically you can thus arouse interest by alluding to things that the pupils are familiar with and appreciate very much. These things may concern football, pop music, etc. If the teacher takes an interest in the spare time interests of his pupils, this will affect the interests of his pupils *vis-à-vis* their teacher and his teaching. This will in its turn create positive attitudes towards school.

Another example of the halo effect is what happens when a teacher who is aware of a pupil's achievement in one subject allows this knowledge to influence his marking in another subject, or when a music teacher is influenced by the pupil's personal behaviour when marking that pupil's knowledge in history of music or his ability to sing. The pupils rightly regard this as unfair and thus it gives them a negative attitude to their school studies.

Perhaps a music teacher more than any other teacher runs the risk of being influenced by halo effects in marking. A music teacher can also easily hide behind the fact that experience of music is to a great extent a question of subjective aesthetic taste. It really is not easy always to decide which one of two singing-voices is the more beautiful.

On the other hand there are more objective viewpoints. For instance when assessing a pupil's ability to keep in tune the teacher should award a high mark if the pupil is able to sing at sight. Not quite as good is the ability to sing a song by heart without the aid of an instrument. Tolerable is to be able to keep in tune if aided by the melody from an instrument. Not being able to sing even if aided by an instrument is not satisfactory. Some of the music fundamentals can be objectively tested by written examinations. Beginners in instrumental music can be at least quantitatively compared on the basis of how much they have accomplished in their first or second instrumental book over a certain period of time. It is advisable to have some such objective measure as a starting point for the marking in order to avoid halo effects. Having considered this, viewpoints concerning beauty of voice, artistic qualities in performance, and so on should be taken into account. (Viewpoints on marking, see also page 75.)

Figure and ground

The figure-ground-relation has been mentioned before as a form-perceptive factor. This factor can also be regarded as an exterior factor of attention. If the teacher is going to demonstrate an object to his class, he must choose a background with a colour contrasting to that of the demonstrated object. The use of coloured chalks is an application of the figure-ground-relation.

This relation can also be regarded as an interior factor of attention, in the way that each individual looks upon himself as a figure against less interesting, 'indistinct', surroundings. In colloquial language we call this egocentricity. A certain amount of egocentricity can be considered sound and is quite synonymous with the concepts of self-esteem and self-respect. The teacher can profit from the pupil's own figure-ground-relation, his egocentricity, by alluding to something that is connected with the pupil's own experiences.

In music education the teacher can assist the establishment of this figure-ground-relation by arranging public and other performances in which the pupil takes an active part. This part need not necessarily be that of a soloist. Membership of a vocal or instrumental ensemble, or of a choir or orchestra, can be equally effective.

The Musical Ear— a Brief Outline

In order to organize our knowledge of the different manifestations of the musical ear[1], it may be useful first to look at a brief skeletal outline. It is convenient to arrange such a table according to two basic principles of disposition.

The first principle of disposition is psycho-physical, i.e., it is based upon the relation between the psychological experience and its physical background, the wave movement, in its different components.

The second principle of disposition is the absolute pitch/relative pitch. It concerns the perception of pitch—and pitch only—as either absolute or relative.

Before going on to details of how the ear interprets the wave movement we shall consider how the sense of absolute or relative pitch affects a musician under various musical circumstances.

Psycho-physical principle of disposition

The components of the musical ear according to this principle concern the perception of:

A   *Pitch*—the musical ear's ability to interpret the fundamental frequency[2] of the wave movement.

B   *Loudness*—the musical ear's ability to interpret the amplitude[2] of the wave movement.

C   *Time*—the musical ear's ability to interpret the duration of a wave movement.

D   *Timbre*—the musical ear's ability to interpret integrally the fundamental frequency and the partials[3] of a wave movement.

E   *Speech-sound*—the musical ear's ability to interpret the so-called formants. These are made up of special frequency groups among the partials. Their separation from the total complex of partials is a matter of resonance, that will be described later together with the whole complex of the phenomenon of partials. It may be questioned whether the perception

---

[1] i.e. the musical abilities of the auditory centre of the brain.
[2] For word explanation see caption to Fig. 13, page 29.
[3] For further explanation see Chapter 4.

of speech-sounds belongs to the musical hearing. It is, however, inevitable that the perception of speech-sound must form part of the faculties of a singer or one who listens to songs. It should also be mentioned that the speech-sounds in concrete and electrophonic music are not used because of their linguistic meaning but as various sound effects.

Absolute—relative principle of disposition[1]

A   *Absolute pitch*—in principle the ability to perceive and name the pitch of a sounded note without being able to compare it with other previously sounded notes. People with absolute pitch define the pitch of a note by its inherent quality, without having recourse to any material of comparison, in the same way as one can distinguish between different colours and decide, for example, that one colour is green without comparing it with red, or yellow, or any other colour. As far as we know at present the acquisition of both absolute and relative pitch depends upon a combination of congenital talent and training.

The absolute pitch can be:

(a) *passive or active*, i.e., the individual can only name a note that has been sounded (passive), *or* he can produce (sing or whistle) any named note (active). In either case no reference to other previously sounded notes is allowed;

(b) *partial or total*, i.e., relate only to the middle part of the pitch range *or* to the total pitch range;

(c) *special or general*, i.e., bear reference to a special instrument *or* relate to all musical instruments independently of qualities.

B   *Regional pitch*—the individual's ability to decide the pitch of a note roughly without having recourse to any note of reference. Everybody possesses regional pitch to some degree. It can be improved by training by which it can be brought closer to absolute pitch.

C   *Standard note pitch*—manifests itself in a violinist's ability to remember the note A and to tune his violin accordingly without reference to any other sound.

[1] Strictly speaking the whole of this second principle could be considered as a subdivision to the psycho-physical principle under the sub-heading of pitch. As will be understood from the chapter on differential psychology, however, there is reason, at least for the time being, to keep the two principles apart.

D   *Relative pitch*—the ability to experience and make comparisons between notes. Relative pitch enables us to recognize a melody irrespective of key-level. If the melody is transposed and thus the key changed the experience of regional pitch will change accordingly, while the relative pitch will recognize the melody as identical.

Absolute and relative pitch as related to musical situations

1 The relative pitch is more indispensable to a musician than the absolute pitch.
2 An individual with absolute pitch normally also has a good relative pitch, but it is not necessarily always perfect.
3 In the case of transposing absolute pitch may cause difficulties.
4 Absolute pitch serves well when learning melodies with difficult intervals.

Nature of the Wave Movement— its Interpretation by the Brain 4

When we speak of wave movement we are usually talking about the movement of water waves. This type of wave movement is called transversal.[1] Characteristic of this kind of wave movement is that the oscillation of the single particles (in this case of water) takes place on a plane perpendicular to the course of the waves. The wave movement which is caught by our hearing is, however, of a different type, the longitudinal. The particles (in this case of air) move back and forth on the same plane as the course of the waves. When we hear a note, it is the result of a regularly increasing and decreasing pressure of longitudinal waves exerted on the ear-drum, that, through the ossicles of the middle ear, the cochlea, and the auditory nerve, is transmitted to the brain. In the cerebral cortex this longitudinal wave movement is transformed and interpreted as sound, i.e., perceived as a sounding note.

In Fig. 13 a transversal and a longitudinal wave movement are so reproduced that they can be compared. It has become customary for practical purposes to illustrate longitudinal waves as if they were transversal. Technical terms such as frequency and amplitude (see caption to Fig. 13) are then easier to understand.

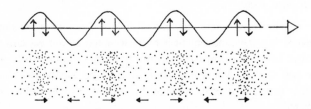

Fig. 13. Longitudinal wave movement (in the bottom of the figure) 'translated' into transversal. The big arrow shows the course of the wave movement. The small arrows show the movements to and fro of the single particles. In the longitudinal wave movement the single particles move horizontally and in the same plane as the course of the wave movement as a whole. In the transversal waves the single particles move vertically. A complete wave (cycle) corresponds to a complete to-and-fro motion of a single particle. The *frequency* of a wave movement is its number of waves (cycles) per second. The *amplitude* is the distance from the middle of the vertical line to the highest point of a transversal wave. The *wave-length* is the distance from crest to crest.

[1] In fact waves on the surface of water are seldom purely transversal, as the wind strikes the surface obliquely. However, waves of the water are transversal enough to serve as an illustration in this context.

The frequency

The terms *number of vibrations,*[1] *waves, cycles, periods per second,* or *number of Herz (Hz)* are all synonyms for frequency and may be used interchangeably. Frequency is interpreted and experienced as pitch by the musical ear. The greater the number of vibrations per second the higher the pitch.

A tuning-fork used to tune the A-string of a violin usually has the frequency of 440 cycles per second (*c/s*). If we multiply this frequency by two we get the frequency of 880 c/s corresponding to A in the nearest higher octave. If we divide by two we get the frequency of 220 corresponding to A in the nearest lower octave. The interval of an octave thus corresponds to a 2 to 1 ratio of frequencies. Actually all intervals have their exact frequency-ratios. For instance the frequency ratio of an exact fifth is 3 to 2 and for a fourth 4 to 3.

It may be recalled that Weber's law refers primarily to loudness; nevertheless it is sometimes used with reference to pitch. This may be justified. The least perceptible difference of frequency is represented by a certain ratio. Thus, in terms of Weber's law the least perceptible difference of frequency (Δs) in relation to the original frequency (s), is a constant ratio, the Weber fraction of pitch. The fraction differs with different individuals. As we shall see later the ability to perceive small differences of pitch and loudness has been used by Seashore and others to test musical talent.

Colour and tone

There are, however, wave movements, which our senses are not able to register. If a wave movement is to be accepted by our ear and transformed to hearing, it must be within the range of about 16 to 20,000 cycles per second. For comparison it may be mentioned that the frequency range of the sense of sight lies within 451–780 million cycles per second.

The idea of some relationship between the experiences of tone and colour is very old. As early as 1704, Newton compared the seven spectral colours (red, orange, yellow, green, blue, indigo, and violet) to the seven notes of the major scale. Newton's theory was abandoned through Helmholtz's criticism in the eighteen-sixties, but the idea of some kind of connection between colour and tone has nevertheless continued to be of interest. Colour instruments have been constructed

---

[1] i.e., complete vibrations oscillating once on each side of the equilibrium, sometimes called 'double vibrations' (*dv*).

to produce colours together with music (Klein, 1932). Special instructions for the use of a colour-instrument has been given by Skriabin (*Prometheus*, 1910). Walt Disney may also be mentioned in this connection for his attempt at making colours express the contents of Bach's *Toccata and Fugue in D minor* (the film *Fantasia*, 1941).

Of special interest in this connection is the coloured hearing, *audition colorée*, which is a type of what is called synesthesia. Synesthesia means that sensations belonging to two different senses are concomitant. In the case of *audition colorée* certain notes, keys, or musical instruments, and certain colours are concomitant. The phenomenon is rare and different with different individuals. Since the concomitant is concerned with the experience of fixed pitch the phenomenon may be considered as a special type of absolute pitch.

Beats

It is of special interest to observe how two simultaneous wave movements are interpreted by the musical ear, when they are nearly, but not quite, of the same frequency; one would naturally expect to hear the two single notes as a dissonance. However, if the frequencies are near enough to one another, only one single note will be heard. This single note will increase and decrease regularly in strength, beat, as many times per second as the difference between the two frequencies.

Listening to beats is very useful when tuning organ pipes. If two organ pipes sound together exactly in tune there are no beats, but as soon as they are the slightest bit apart beats occur, and the more apart they are, the more beats are heard.

On the other hand beats are used as a special effect in the organ stop called *vox humana* or *voix céleste*. In this organ stop each note is sounded by two pipes so tuned that they produce the desired beats.

A piano-tuner uses equal temperament (see page 39). The rate of beats between the notes in fourths and fifths enables him to determine the correct proportion of necessary deviation from the acoustic fourths and fifths of the overtone series.

Difference and summation tones

We have seen that a condition for the occurrence of beats is that the two simultaneous vibrations are close together in frequency. When they are not close enough to produce beats, another phenomenon may occur: difference tones. The difference tone is experienced as a note of a frequency corresponding to the difference between the two original simultaneous frequencies.

The phenomenon has been used in the lowest parts of certain organ stops. These very low notes would need extremely large pipes. Instead of using such big pipes, two smaller pipes are used for each note. The two smaller pipes are tuned to produce the required pitch as a difference tone.

Analogous to difference tones a summation tone is experienced as a note corresponding to the sum of the frequencies of two simultaneous wave movements.

Both difference and summation tones may be heard on a piano. For example if the notes D and A are played simultaneously one may be able to hear as a difference tone the D of the octave below. The same fifth may produce as a summation tone F sharp in the octave above.

String players, who tune their strings in pure fifths, are aided by difference tones. The difference tone of a fifth is exactly one octave below the lower note of the fifth. If the fifth is not exactly pure, the difference tone in the lower octave is more out of tune than the two original notes of the fifth. This is fundamentally the same thing that we have discussed earlier in connection with Weber's law. To the total impression of the fifth out of tune, plus the difference tone still more out of tune, is added the possibility of hearing beats as an extra aid in tuning a string instrument.

Amplitude

Amplitude (see also Fig. 13, page 29) is interpreted by the musical ear as loudness. The classification and estimation of loudness in music is very subjective. Expressions such as *piano*, *forte*, *fortissimo*, and the like give considerable liberty to the performer. For scientific purposes an objective unit of loudness is needed. Such a unit is the decibel, i.e., the tenth of a bel. The unit is named after A. G. Bell, the inventor of the telephone. It represents about the smallest perceptible change in loudness. Since the science of electronics with all its advanced technical aids, has entered into the creation and performance of music it is necessary to use objective standards of loudness, at least in some modern music.

Mention of the decibel has arisen from discussion about Weber's law. This law has also been differently formulated by Fechner, who found loudness to be a logarithmic function. Thus the Fechner formula is:

$$n = C \log s,$$

where C is the constant number 10, s the stimulus measured by physical units of energy[1], and n the loudness measured by decibel.

[1] The energy producing the wave movement may be expressed in terms of electricity. Thus a decibel may also be defined as the loudness produced by an energy of 10^{-16} W/cm^2, i.e., one ten thousandth of a billionth watt per square centimetre at a frequency of 1000 cycles per second.

The loudness at the threshold of hearing is usually taken as zero point of the decibel scale. The intensity of a stimulus producing that threshold is the corresponding unit of physical energy in the application of the Fechner formula below[1].

Units of physical energy (intensity)	Application of the Fechner formula	Units of psychical experience of loudness measured by decibel
1	10 . log 1 = 10.0	0
1·2589	10 . log 1·2589 = 10.0·1	1
10	10 . log 10 = 10.1	10
100	10 . log 100 = 10.2	20
1000	10 . log 1000 = 10.3	30
10000	10 . log 10000 = 10.4	40

Explanation and examples of the application of the Fechner formula could be more detailed. However, the given facts are enough to show that while the psychologically experienced decibels can be reckoned in terms of addition (10 dB [10 dB = 20 dB) the corresponding physical units of energy must be reckoned in terms of multiplication (10 phys. units × 10 phys. units = 100).

To give two examples of loudness, a whisper at a distance of four feet is experienced as a loudness of about 20 dB, and a motor-car, not raced, at a distance of a few yards gives about 50 dB. Above 115 dB is in the neighbourhood of the threshold of pain.

The limits of the area of hearing can be measured by an audiometer. The result is obtained in an audiogram showing all the frequencies that can be heard. The audiogram also shows the thresholds of hearing, i.e., the smallest amplitude that is necessary for the different frequencies within the area to be heard. The upper limit of the amplitudes shows the threshold of pain. Hearing is normally found to be most keen in the area between 1000 and 5000 cycles.

In addition to the decibel we also use the unit phon. At a frequency of 1000 cycles the two units (phon and decibel) may be taken to be the same thing. Sensitivity to loudness, however, is different at different levels of frequency. The unit phon is corrected to these differences, which is not the case with decibels. These differences become greater the nearer one approaches the limits of the area of hearing. For instance

[1] A reader who is not acquainted with logarithms may be relieved to know that they can be found in arithmetical tables just like squares, or square roots, and certain other numbers. It is beyond the scope of this book to give a detailed algebraic explanation.

3

at a frequency of 200 cycles 53 dB equals only 40 phons. An interesting conclusion from research about the area of hearing and the necessity of the phon as a unit of loudness, is that our hearing is most sensitive to faint sound, and also least tolerant of excessive sound, in the range of the upper half of the piano. Bass music needs more energy than, for example, a piccolo.

Complexity of the wave movement

The wave movement produced by a musical instrument—electronic generators excluded—is complex. The string, or the column of air in a wind instrument, does not vibrate only in its entirety but simultaneously divides into several small vibrating sections. This division always occurs in 'whole' sections, i.e., a string does not divide into $2\frac{1}{2}$ or $3\frac{1}{2}$ sections but into 2, 3, 4, 5, etc., sections. Thus the resulting sectional-vibrations, partials, constitute a series of partials with predictable partial-frequencies, once the frequency of the original wave movement (i.e., the fundamental frequency) is known.

Timbre

Timbre (quality of tone) is the interpretation of the partials as a whole by the musical ear. Different instruments and voices produce different experiences of this totality depending on the strength of the different partials characterizing the complexity of their wave movements. Thanks to partial-analysis the partial-spectra of different instruments are now known in detail. This has made possible imitation of different instruments and organ stops in the electronic organs. Also quite new tone-qualities may be produced.

The overtone-series

Although the series of partials is experienced only as timbre by the musical ear and never as a corresponding series of overtones or a kind of chord of overtones, the concept of an overtone-series is often used and illustrated as in Fig. 14. With some concentration a single partial may well be heard as an overtone but never a whole series.

Resonance

When a vibration reaches a new medium, this new medium may reflect the vibration (echo) or absorb (kill) the vibration. It may also happen that a sympathetic vibration is originated and in that case we speak of

34

resonance. Finally it may happen that the sympathetic vibration is reflected to and fro between the 'walls' of the new medium. If this stationary wave is fed with new vibrations of the original frequency, the stationary wave will be amplified very quickly and the amplitudes of the new waves will be added to the amplitude of the stationary wave.

Fig. 14. The lower tones of an overtone-series based on the note C.

Thus the new medium will quickly become a new and stronger source of sound than the original one. This is the usual way to reinforce the sound of musical instruments.

The violin may serve as an example. If we want to play softly on the violin we may diminish the pressure of the bow. In this case we diminish both the original intensity and the reinforcement of the resonance. We may also play with the mute on. In that case the intensity is diminished through weakening of the resonance independently of the bow.

Finally if we play the violin without a sound box (body), we get an extremely faint sound because the intensity of the strings is not at all reinforced.

Speech sounds

Reinforcement by resonance is important in speech. The vocal cords are in themselves very weak sources of sound. These sounds are reinforced by resonance in the mouth and other cavities above the vocal cords, and by bones in the head.

The following is what happens when a vowel is sounded:

(i) The speaker 'thinks' a speech sound.
(ii) The vocal cords are set in motion and give off a wave movement, containing the whole complex of basic vibration and partials.
(iii) Above the vocal cords certain stationary wave movements are started and these are quickly reinforced, i.e., resonance is rendered effective.
(iv) The frequencies of the stationary vibrations consist of a selection of partials called formants.

35

(v) Which of all possible formants are used is settled by the speaker adjusting his mouth-cavity and articulation in such a way that only the desired partials are reinforced to become formants.[1]

(vi) The selected formants now become a reinforced secondary source of vibrations. These formant vibrations pass on to the ears of the speaker and other possible listeners and are interpreted by the human brain as a vowel. Each speech sound thus is originated by its special corresponding formants.

The first two formants for the speech sound *e*, as in *sea*, are in the frequency-fields of 350 and 2200 c/s. For *a*, as in *last*, the two lowest formants are 700 and 1000 c/s.

Also the consonants have their characteristic fields of frequency. The widest range of frequency is that of the *sh*-sound. This sound is a 'white' sound in the sense that it is originated by a complex of frequencies from the whole area of hearing, just as white colour is originated by a mixture of all frequencies of light waves.

Through modern technical aids the frequency-fields of all different speech sounds can be mapped out in sound spectra. By such means phonetics has become an exact science, where speech can be analysed and also synthetically produced.

The vocal cords are not always at work when producing a speech sound. For instance, the breathed consonants, as well as the whisper, are produced without the aid of the vocal cords. This shows that the formants can be originated without the activity of the vocal cords. When the vocal cords are active the speech sound is voiced. Otherwise it is unvoiced.

A general rule in voice training is to keep to the head register. The feeling of relief when a note is produced with the head register compared to 'sung in the throat' is no doubt technically due to the fact that the singer in the former case gets most of the loudness for nothing as a result of reinforcement through resonance.

Sine-tones

A sine-tone is produced by a wave movement that lacks partial-vibrations and mathematically corresponds to a sine curve (see Fig. 15). These notes are thus pure tones without what we normally regard as timbre. They are used in some tests of musical talent and are the material of *electronic music*. The sounds of this kind of music are produced in electronic tone generators. The vibrations produced by the

[1] The frequencies of the reinforced formants and the corresponding partials of the fundamental of the vocal cords need not coincide exactly. A reinforcement of a formant-frequency is brought about, even if the partial-frequency is just in the neighbourhood.

generators can be simultaneously combined to imitate the timbre of common musical instruments, but the great advantage of the electronic generators is, of course, the possibilities of producing quite new sounds.

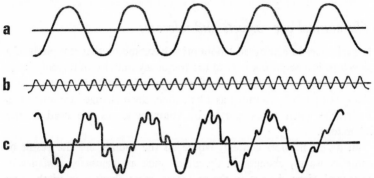

Fig. 15. Two sine waves (*a*, *b*) and a complex wave (*c*). *a* is the sine wave corresponding to the lasting tone of a tuning-fork. When a tuning-fork is hit with a hammer on the top of one of the prongs, there is produced a clang tone by the superposition of the two sine waves *a* and *b*, resulting in the complex curve *c*. After a very short while the clang tone is reduced to a pure tone, i.e., only the sine wave *a* is lasting, while *b* has disappeared.

Tone generators of a simple construction are often available in the physical laboratories of schools. They may be used in combination with tape recorders in laboratory music lessons. Why should not the pupils of an electronic age try to create some electronic sounds as well as conventional music?

Electronic music is often confused with *concrete music*. Concrete music, like electronic, is tape recorded. However, concrete music is not produced on electronic generators but is recorded from the concrete world of sound. All kinds of sounds may be used such as the noise of a plater's shop, the braking of a tram-car; also the sound of a human voice, or a conventional instrument. Having recorded a supply of different sounds the composer treats his material in different ways—cutting, sticking, choosing rate of speed—to suit his composition. This may also be done in a music laboratory lesson.[1]

[1] As an instance we may take the task of producing 'water music'. As an introduction water-inspired conventional music such as Chopin's *Prelude of Rain-Drops*, Duke Ellington's *Night and Day*, or something similar may be mentioned and played. Some song on the theme of rain or water may be sung. The next phase in the lesson will be the collecting of water sounds such as raining water, dropping water, water waves, water poured into a glass, water out of a water-tap, etc. Then comes the treatment of the tapes: cutting, sticking, putting sounds together in successive, and simultaneous, combinations, choosing rate of speed, etc. Finally, the concrete composition may be put into a greater context serving as an interesting feature of a programme on water, together with other water music, songs and pictures of waterfalls, lakes, film of a ship in storm, etc. Lessons of this kind may be used as a group work, or part of an integrated team work between teachers of different school subjects. (See page 105.)

Sometimes electronic and concrete music are mixed in one and the same composition. The music thus created must not be called either electronic or concrete but *electrophonic*.

The musical ear corrects and tolerates

Experiments in acoustical laboratories have shown that the pitch of a sine-tone is a result not only of the frequency but also of the amplitude of the sound wave. Quite small changes of amplitude may cause a change of pitch by as much as a half-tone. Such changes are much less noticeable when notes caused by complex waves are used in the laboratory.

In a real musical context, where all the sounds are the result of complex waves, changes in dynamics such as *crescendo, diminuendo, forte,* and *piano,* do not in themselves suggest changes in pitch. The musical ear always perceives pitch with tolerations and corrections in favour of a musical context as far as the deviations from the expected pitch are within a certain small range. Other examples of this remarkable adaptability of pitch-hearing are the tolerance of equal temperament (page 39), and beats (page 31), as well as the vocal and instrumental *vibrato*.

The vibrato

The *vibrato* is a periodic pulsation of pitch above and below the note in the score. The listener does not experience this as a really pulsating pitch but as an even mean pitch between the top and the bottom of the pulsation. It is experienced as adding to the richness, flexibility, and tenderness of the music. There is also a simultaneous pulsation of loudness and timbre.

Seashore and co-workers have made close investigations of vocal and instrumental *vibratos*. The individual variations of the extent of the vocal *vibrato* were quite marked, but three-quarters of the examined singers had a *vibrato* of about a half-tone. The pitch *vibratos* of violinists were on an average smaller than those of the singers and of about a quarter-tone. The rate of speed of the *vibratos* varied among the 29 examined singers from 5·9 to 7·8 *vibratos* per second.

Tutors of the violin often recommend that the pupils wait to use the *vibrato* until they have practised for some years. The early use of the *vibrato* is supposed to endanger their ability to play in tune. The danger of this is, however, probably overemphasized. Why should the practice of listening to a mean pitch of a *vibrato* be more dangerous to playing in tune than the practice of listening to a pitch without *vibrato*? What hinders beginners from playing in tune is certainly not ears spoilt for pitch by *vibrato* but very understandable difficulties of coordination between eye, ear, bow, and fingering. Mastering these difficulties takes time, during which the pupil may be allowed to play a little out of tune now and then. If the pupil happens to start using *vibrato* during this period of practice he may as well be allowed or even encouraged to do so. Many pupils at once find that their instruments sound really 'violinistic' and are stimulated to go on with their practice more willingly. The desired coordination between ear and fingering will come eventually, if the pupil has got an ear for pitch. If he lacks ear for pitch, practice will be useless whether with or without *vibrato*.

Equal temperament

If we want our music to allow modulations from any key to another we must also—as will be shown below—allow our music to be slightly out of tune. This problem became apparent through the development of multi-part music in the seventeenth century. During the first half of the eighteenth century Johann Sebastian Bach advocated equal temperament as the best solution; the system is still being used. In order to prove that all keys could be used with the new system he wrote his well-known 48 preludes and fugues, *Das wohltemperierte Klavier*. Before the time of Bach, however, the equal temperament had been proposed as early as 1542 by the Spaniard, Bartolo Rames. In 1636 the French mathematician Mersenne had published the frequency ratios of the new system and in 1691 still another spokesman, the German organ builder Andreas Werckmeister, appeared.

Music perfectly in tune must use a fifth that is acoustically correct, i.e., the corresponding frequency ratio must be 3:2. If such fifths are built upon each other they will in turn become key notes in keys with more and more sharps. We thus get the series C–G–D–A–E–B–F♯–C♯–G♯–D♯–A♯–E♯–B♯. The note B♯ being key note of the B♯-scale with 12 sharps as key signature, ought to be identical with the original C, but that is not the case. We find a difference between B♯ and C of about a quarter of a half-tone above C. This difference is called the 'comma of Pythagoras' and apparently is big enough to prevent us from modulating at will among the keys.

Equal temperament is so tuned that each fifth in the series of fifths mentioned above is exactly so much out of tune, that the inaccuracy is equally shared by the twelve keys. B♯ becomes identical with C. The comma of Pythagoras is divided into twelve equal parts.

String and wind players sometimes deviate from equal temperament. We sometimes think of these deviations as being better in tune than the intervals of equal temperament. However, research in this field does not altogether confirm this opinion. An investigation by Arnold Small in 1937 of twelve recordings of violinists rather points to the contrary. Deviations from the tempered scale intervals were found to an extent of 0·05 tone or more over 50% of the time. Deviations of more than 0·1 tone or more occurred about 25% of the time. Looking for special tendencies from the tempered major scale he found that the most common deviation was for the leading note (the seventh) to be raised (85%) and the subdominant (fourth) to be lowered (80%). Other common deviations were contraction of minor and diminished intervals (51%) as well as expansion of major and augmented intervals (44%). Deviations as to chromatics showed a tendency to over-shoot the alteration in the direction of the chromatic used.

The deviations from the tempered scale are thus not always in accordance with the divisions of the Pythagorean scale. They may be equally explained as a matter of the logic of cadence and an attempt to sharpen or flatten intervals according to the tendency of the melodic movement. Inconvenient fingering and change of position of the left hand may also accidentally be of some consequence.

Whether equal temperament or deviations from equal temperament are preferred, it is obvious that the musical ear corrects and tolerates minute deviations of pitch in favour of the musical context.

Test Psychology

5

The origin of intelligence testing

One of the most important aids in modern research is *statistics*. By using statistics individual errors can be eliminated and psychology thus has the means of finding out with some exactitude the characteristics and abilities of the average man. Once this has been achieved the individual may be compared to the average. This is what happens in the construction and use of psychological tests.

The French physician Alfred Binet was, in 1905, the first scientist to construct an intelligence test. He did it at the request of the school authorities in Paris. They wanted a device that would enable them to decide whether children should be directed to special remedial classes. Binet used mental age (MA) as a measure of intelligence. A child who is ten years old has a chronological age (CA) of ten. When tested he may show achievements corresponding to those of an average child of the age of eleven. In that case his mental age (MA) is 11. If his achievements instead were below average he might have an MA of 9.

The German psychologist, William Stern, realized that MA was an imperfect measure of intelligence, as the development of one year meant more at a younger age than at a later. He proposed the use of *Intelligence Quotient* (IQ) as a measure, which has since been accepted all over the world. The formula for the calculation of IQ is

$$IQ = \frac{MA}{CA} \cdot 100.$$

The factor 100 has been added to the formula in order to avoid decimal numbers.

The structure of intelligence

The concept of intelligence has always been difficult to define. Earlier psychologists defined intelligence as the ability to solve problems without the aid of former experience. Nowadays very often an *operative* way of defining is used. Intelligence is what is operating when a person is tested by an intelligence test. According to this view one refers to the particular test which has been used when one states a person's IQ.

The continued research on intelligence has been aimed at mapping the structure of intelligence with the aid of the advanced statistical technique of *factorial analysis*. This research, with the Englishman Spearman and the American Thurstone as leading names, has come to the conclusion that intelligence is not a uniform function but consists of several different factors. Thus there are two verbal factors accounting for linguistic talent. The ability of spatial imagination is represented by a spatial factor. Other factors are concerned with perceptual, numerical, and logical abilities. Among remaining factors a factor of memory should also be mentioned. The results of factorial analysis indicate that IQ in many situations must be considered an insufficient measure of intelligence, and thus ought to be supplemented by a profile chart of achievements in different factors.

Musical aptitude and factorial analysis

The method of factorial analysis is now also being used in the field of music psychology. A prerequisite of this method is, of course, the availability of tests of musical aptitude. Pioneers in the testing of musical aptitude are, among others, Seashore and Gordon (USA), Wing and Bentley (England), and Franklin and Holmström (Sweden). We will return to their test constructions in a later context.

Among the pioneers in factorial analysis of musical aptitude may be mentioned Karlin (USA), McLeish and Wing (England), and Franklin and Holmström (Sweden). Summarizing, and somewhat modifying, the results and discussions of different researches one finds that these are mostly concerned with the sense of pitch probably consisting of two co-operant factors. One factor is considered to be of an acoustic character and physiologically and genetically demarcated. The second factor should be a factor of experience of pitch in the musical context. So far as is known no factorial analysis study has been made involving absolute pitch.

Reliability and validity

When constructing a test it is essential to revise and improve the construction until the test has a satisfactory degree of *reliability* and *validity*. Reliability is the test's correlation, co-variation, with itself, i.e., to what degree a test is consistent, or gives the same result when used a second time on the same subjects. Validity is the correlation of a test with other criteria considered to measure the same variable (personal traits, knowledge, intelligence, musical aptitude, etc.) as the test. The degree of validity thus shows whether a test is measuring what it is supposed to measure and nothing else.

Different formulae are used to calculate *correlations* to show the degree of relationship between two variables, but they all give as a measure a coefficient varying between $+1$ and -1. $+1$ means the more of one variable the more of the other. -1 means the more of one variable the less of the other. The coefficient o means no relationship at all between the two variables. For example, height of fathers correlates 0·56 with height of sons (McNemar, 1955). An example of negative correlation is found between number of hours of practice on a typewriter and number of typing errors made in a test, i.e., the more practice the fewer mistakes. Correlations are not percentages and they do not imply causality but only magnitude and direction of relationship. The significance of correlation is probably best understood by comparing instances of correlation in the following context.

The reliability of a test should be high. An intelligence test must have a reliability of at least 0·90. The reliability can be computed as the correlation between two sets of scores when a group of subjects are given the same test on two occasions. Another available method is the split-half method. The items of the test are divided into two halves, with the odd-numbered items in one, and the even in the other. The two 'split halves' are then correlated in combination with a statistical device to make the correlation comparable to the figure obtained if two full-length tests had been used. A way to secure a higher reliability coefficient is to increase the number of items in the test. On the other hand a test must not be allowed to take too much time.

School marks are often used as criteria for calculating the *validity* of a test of intelligence. However, the expected figures need not be so high as in the case of reliability. A validity of 0·60 is considered quite sufficient in view of the fact that success at school very much depends on factors other than intelligence, e.g., diligence. If the validity is *too* low it may go together with a low reliability, for if a test has a low reliability, i.e., correlation with itself, it must also have low correlations with other criteria.

Standardizing

Calculating reliability and validity are essential procedures in standardizing a test. Also statistically calculated norms must be produced to show what the average person of a certain age is expected to perform.

When these norms are produced the individual can be tested and compared to the norms. However, it has to be remembered that, while the test may have been most carefully constructed, the individual subject is not always consistent. The risk of the subject's being nervous, tired, or having an aversion to the test, etc., can never be totally avoided. This must always be borne in mind when interpreting test results.

In spite of observed imperfections of tests and procedures of testing, statistically based tests are not only most important but quite indispensable means of psychological research. Testing also has a wide range of practical application in vocational guidance and educational systems. When directing a pupil to remedial classes the influence of intelligence testing has often been overemphasized. It has been forgotten that the test was given as a result of a teacher's report, founded on long observation of the pupil; this is as important as the test result. So the test is only complementary to a judgment that otherwise would have been made solely by the teacher.

What has been said about intelligence tests, their reliability, validity, and usefulness, is, of course, applicable to tests of musical aptitude. The demands of reliability and validity must be as keenly observed. When interpreting individual results the possibilities of error in individual cases must be taken into consideration. Among the reasons for error— especially with young children—is the fact that different degrees of musical knowledge and experience influence the ability to understand the test instruction. Also the capability of concentrating on test items is very different with young children and usually can only be depended upon for a short period of time. For these reasons a test result should not be the only criterion, for instance, as to whether a child is to take lessons or not on an instrument. When the child has had practice for some time, however, a test can be useful as a complement to the teacher's report if deciding whether to continue the music studies or not. One must also bear in mind that success in music studies, as in other studies, depends not only on aptitude, but also on diligence, carefulness, and other characteristics that are not tested.

Testing of musical aptitude

There are two principles used in constructing tests of musical aptitude. Some test constructors keep to one or the other principle and some conveniently use both principles or disregard them for practical purposes or scientific reasons. However, the principles are very useful in describing any of the tests.

The first principle is psycho-physical, corresponding to the first principle mentioned in Chapter 3 concerning the musical ear. The different components of the sound wave are perceived as pitch, loudness, time, and timbre. These components of musical aptitude are tested one

44

at a time, while the other components are kept constant. This is also the general technique of a variable-experiment, following the old standard 'rule of one variable', to keep all conditions constant except for one single factor, which is the experimental factor.

The most outstanding representative of the psycho-physical principle is C. E. Seashore.

The second principle disregards the acoustic origin of sound. According to this principle, musical aptitude should be measured as musically as possible, i.e., in a musical context. Pitch, for example, is not usually experienced in isolation but in the succession of notes in a melody, or simultaneously in a chord, or most commonly in a melody with chords. This principle is maintained by H. D. Wing. It is not quite analogous to the second principle used in the outline of Chapter 3. However, it certainly does interest itself in relative pitch just as much as it lacks interest in wave movement.

Since the test batteries[1] of Seashore and Wing are typical of the two mentioned principles, they will be examined in detail. In addition, two Swedish test constructions will be presented, as well as two batteries of the nineteen-sixties—one English and one American—intended to be more suitable for young children.

Seashore

As has been mentioned above the Seashore battery is constructed to measure the factors of musical talent one at a time, while the others are held constant. Thus, while the sense of pitch is tested with the aid of fifty pairs of frequencies, all the other components of the wave movement, i.e., amplitude, duration, and complexity, are kept constant. The complexity is kept constant by using sine waves produced in a tone generator. The experimental situation is thus controlled in order to be sure that the sense of pitch is tested and nothing else.

When listening to fifty pairs of pitch sounds, O[2] has to state in the case of each pair of notes, whether the second note is higher or lower than the first.

The sense of pitch having been tested, the sense of loudness is tested in a similar way but this time the amplitude is varied so that the second note in a pair to be perceived has more or less loudness than the first. Of course in this test the frequency is kept constant together with the other factors of the sound wave.

Similarly O's ability to make judgments of note lengths is tested.

The sense of timbre is tested with the aid of fifty pairs of timbres.

---

[1] Battery, i.e., a system consisting of several tests, each test having several items.
[2] O, a tested subject, a common notation in psychological literature.

These are produced by complex waves having the same basic frequency of 180 cycles per second and in addition to this the five lowest partials. The third and fourth partials are sometimes changed and O has to decide whether a change of timbre has occurred or not.

The perception of speech sound is not included in the Seashore battery,[1] although he has shown some interest in the analysis of vowel quality in other contexts.

Seashore's test of tonal memory may be described as a test of the immediate memory span of pitch. As in the special pitch test, sine tones are used and the sequences of tones are atonal, i.e., cannot be referred to any conventional key. Although published as long ago as 1919, the material of this test is obviously very modern being both electronic and atonal in design. The process of testing is that O listens to thirty paired tone sequences of the length of three to five tones. When a sequence is played the second time O has to decide which of the tones has been altered.

The results in the different tests can be compared with a percentile scale showing how many per cent of pupils of a certain age are able to accomplish a certain result.

The Seashore battery has been subject to much criticism. The frequency differences in the pitch test are said to be too small to have relevance to a musical context. The smallest differences are only two cycles. Criticism of this kind may be compared to what has been said in Chapter 4 about beats, *vibrato*, and equal temperament. Apparently the musical ear tolerates, or corrects, minute differences of pitch in favour of a musical context. Other criticism aims at the sine tones.[2] Most of the individuals tested are not accustomed to notes without timbre, so they get a worse result than would be expected, especially on the test of pitch. The reliability and validity of the separate tests are not considered entirely satisfactory, with the possible exception of the test of memory. If tested twice the second testing quite often gives the individual a better result. This may be a result of the subject's getting more acquainted with, for example, the sound of the sine tones on the second testing. In such a case Seashore even recommends that a subject should be tested twice with the first rather easy part of the pitch test before proceeding to the second part. This implies that the administrator of the test should check the result after the first half has been completed, in order to find out whether the subject has adjusted himself to the test situation or not.[3]

[1] Nor is it included in any other battery of tests of musical aptitude as far as the author knows.

[2] See also footnote on page 114.

[3] The fact that this probably very seldom is done is no doubt one of the causes of the low degree of reliability found when retesting with the pitch test.

Seashore has also pointed out that his battery is not capable of testing all aspects of musical talent, but he maintains, on the other hand, that there is no way to test the subjective aspects of musicality objectively.

Finally it may be said that if a test *is* to be based on the psycho-physical principle, there is hardly any other way to do it than the Seashore way, from a logical point of view. However, if one abandons the psycho-physics quite different solutions present themselves as we shall see.

Wing

The Wing battery consists of one group of tests of a rather elementary and objective kind, and another group of four tests of a more subjective, musical kind.

The first test of the first group is a test on chord analysis. The subject has to decide how many notes there are in a chord. The easiest chord has only one note, the more difficult ones several notes combined in different ways.

The second test in the elementary group is concerned with pitch analysis. The subject has to decide whether a note in a chord moves or not when the chord is played a second time. If it moves O has to indicate whether the movement is up or down.

The third test is a test of tonal memory. A sequence of notes, a melody, is played twice. The second time a note is changed and the subject has to state the number of the note that is changed in the sequence.

This first group of tests is intended to be used as early as the age of eleven. The four remaining tests must be used with greater caution. In these tests the subject has to decide which of two performances of the same piece of music is best harmonized, phrased, and accented, etc. The constructor has used well-known melodies and pieces of music. The composer's own version, considered as the better one, is to be compared with the constructor's more or less impaired version.

Contrary to Seashore, Wing uses piano notes. Wing also differs from Seashore as to the technique of the variable experiment, i.e., he disregards the rule of one variable at a time. For instance, the sense of pitch is tested in chords, where a sense of consonance and dissonance, leading notes, etc., may influence the result, in addition to the sense of pitch, when two chords are sounded in succession. The melodies in the tonal memory test are not atonal, which means that the result may be influenced by tonal melodic associations. Furthermore the notes are not of equal length, so it is not quite a question of immediate memory span of a number of notes but also a question of the sense of rhythm involved in the test. However, Wing is as logical in his approach as Seashore in his. If the musical principle of testing is to be used—and this principle only—one must admit that the isolated factors of psychophysical tests are rarely, if ever, encountered in real music.

Like Seashore's, the Wing battery is recorded and thus is intended for use as a group test, i.e., several subjects may be tested at the same time. Wing's tests are standardized but the norms are more broadly outlined than those of Seashore.

Holmström

Holmström's battery consists of four tests, three of which have the same design as the three of the elementary Wing group. A rhythmic melodic test has been added in order to satisfy the necessity of testing the sense of rhythm. Holmström's battery is a group test and has been frequently used in schools of instrumental music.

Bentley

Bentley's battery is intended for children from seven to twelve years of age. It consists of four tests and may be considered a compromise between the Seashore- and Wing-type. It is of use as a group test but Bentley recommends that it be used only individually with children of the age of seven.

The first test is concerned with the sense of pitch. It is produced on the same principle as Seashore's test of pitch. Bentley uses twenty pairs of sine tones which the subject has to decide about as to pitch. The differences of pitch extend from half a tone to about one ninth of a half-tone.

The second test is a test of tonal memory. It uses ten melodies of five notes each played on a pipe organ. The use of a musical instrument is on the Wing principle. Bentley, however, is more in favour of the principle of one factor at a time, keeping all notes constant as to length and strength.

The third test is a test of chord analysis. O has to decide the number of notes in a chord played on a pipe organ. The design is that of Wing, although the notes of a pipe organ are of a more constant loudness than those of a piano.

The fourth test is a test of rhythmic memory. O is to compare the performance of two rhythms played on a pipe organ. Pitch and loudness are kept constant in the items, which is a Seashore principle.

Bentley regrets that the reliability of the tests ($r = 0.84$) is somewhat lower than desirable because of their rather few items. However, he finds a compromise necessary because of children's inability to concentrate for longer periods of time. The whole battery of sixty items takes 21 minutes, and is recorded on a gramophone record.

Gordon

Like Bentley's battery of 1966, Gordon's of 1965 has profited by using and improving techniques of former test constructors.

Gordon's battery consists of tests in the three groups of Tonal Imagery, Rhythm Imagery, and Musical Sensitivity. The first group is concerned with melody and harmony, the second with tempo and metre, and the third phrasing, balance, and style.

The tests in principle are somewhat similar to the second group of four tests in the Wing battery. Contrary to Wing, however, Gordon has composed the music examples himself and they are performed by a professional violinist and cellist.

The tests are recorded and usable as group tests with children from the age of nine up to sixteen.

Franklin

As has been shown in one of Franklin's items on page 19 the subject has to fill in the last note in an unfinished melody. The test belongs to the musical type. The subject must show a good sense of pitch and logic of tonal harmony in order to achieve a good performance. In its published version as an individual, not standardized, test, with acceptable reliability and validity, it has been used in factorial analysis. It may also be used for practical purposes in testing ability to keep in tune, e.g., when selecting singers for a choir.

Other tests

The tests mentioned have been described in terms of the two principles of psycho-physics and musical context. Other test constructors such as Whistler and Thorpe, Drake, Kwalwasser and Dykema, Colwell, and several others, could be mentioned but the examples chosen serve to illustrate the two types and some variations.

In this context it must be added that testing of musical aptitude is not always enough for the purpose of vocational guidance. For a virtuoso, for instance, motor and perceptual speed is of the utmost importance, as is memory of muscle movement. A composer must have a good general intelligence and cultural background. A piano-tuner must be able to hear the rate of beats and also be able to adjust the mechanism of a piano.

Besides tests of aptitude there are also tests of personality traits as well as standardized tests of knowledge in school subjects and other achievements.

The personality tests are intended to reveal different personal traits, e.g., if a person is neurotic, extroverted, or introverted. Such a test may consist of systematically designed questions as in the MMPI test (Minnesota Multiphasic Personality Inventory), which, like other personality tests, has been much used in psychiatry. Other methods of testing personality are the projective techniques. These techniques are designed in such a way that the subject reveals his thoughts and feelings, that is 'projects himself', when making fantasies about ink-blots (the Rorschach test, named after its constructor), or interpreting pictures (Murray's Thematic Apperception Test, TAT).

Standardized tests on school children are often used in subjects like English and arithmetic. They could also be of use in history of music and art, as well as in the terminology of elementary music—as far as one needs a standardized measure of knowledge. Conservatoires and Academies of music have their own, usually home-made and not standardized, tests of different kinds to select their applicants for admission.

Disregarding tests of knowledge and achievement, it has no doubt been the ambition of test constructors to devise tests that are wholly independent of experience and musical knowledge. Aptitude has been defined earlier as an inherited ability to solve problems, react to pitch, etc. Since, however, gains in IQ have been detected during the years of growth and after some years of study the definition of aptitude is no longer satisfactory, one must doubt the possibilities of making a test wholly independent of experience. Conclusions that may be drawn are also very much dependent upon the different test constructions that are used. So let us confirm that musical aptitude, as defined at the beginning of this chapter concerning intelligence, should be operational. The particular test used should be stated as the measure of musical aptitude found on a particular occasion in the life of an individual, remembering that the result could be affected partly by heredity, partly by experience, partly by fatigue, etc. Let us bear this in mind when we consider the problem of nature and nurture with regard to musical aptitude.

Heredity of musical aptitude

The study of twins is probably the most practicable source of any conclusions about the question of nature and nurture. Identical twins are of special interest since they have identical hereditary factors. In comparing influence of heredity and environment on personality one must, however, also remember that environment is experienced as both objective and subjective. An environment is, of course, objective *per se* but as it is experienced differently by different individuals it becomes for these individuals a more or less subjective experience. The influence of environment is, however, most objectively measured in the case of identical twins who have shared the same environment since birth.

Comparisons between identical twins who have, on one hand, grown up together, and, on the other, grown up in different environments, will thus give many indications of the influence of heredity and environment on different personal traits. In the case of intelligence it has been found that heredity is a strong factor, but only a good environment will allow hereditary factors their full development. For instance, good teaching and diligent study over a period of time tend to increase the tested intelligence of children.

Research concerning the heredity of musical aptitude is still rare. An older Norwegian and a modern English investigation may be of interest.

The Norwegians, A. and F. Mjöen, together with H. Koch, used an elaborate inquiry, testing both children and their parents. The investigation showed a clear heredity with regard to musical aptitude but not the ways in which the aptitude was inherited.

Rosamund Shuter in England has reported an investigation of about fifty pairs of twins between the ages of nine and sixteen years. They were tested with the Wing battery. The identical twins showed higher correlations of musical aptitude than the non-identical, which certainly indicates hereditarian influence. Five of the pairs of identical twins who had grown up in different environments all got higher scores than the average. The twins in two of these pairs had a hardly noticeable difference of scores, while there were more noticeable differences observed in the other three pairs. Shuter has also tried to calculate from test results and correlations how many of the co-variations can be attributed to heredity or environment respectively. Her figures show 42% hereditarian influence in the whole material, and 62% if only boys are taken into account. The figures must, of course, be treated with a certain reservation considering the limitations of the statistical material. They should also be seen against the background of what has been said above about the difficulties of defining musical aptitude and of constructing tests independent of the subject's experience.

Psychology of Learning 6

In the psychology of learning experiments with animals have been extensively used. The reason for this is that the learning of animals is less complicated than that of human beings because their nervous system is less highly developed. So the fundamental patterns of learning can be more easily discovered and investigated. A number of animals of the same species should be used for statistical reasons. An experiment can be easily repeated by different researchers under equal conditions. Of course, experiments with human subjects are also made. Most theories of learning, however, are based upon experiments with animals, so a survey of learning theories had better begin with a description of some classical examples of these experiments.

Pavlov

The experiments of the Russian physiologist Pavlov on dogs, at the turn of the century, have become world-famous both in medical and psychological science. Pavlov found that a hungry dog produces saliva at the *sight* of food, i.e., before the food actually reaches his mouth. From this he drew the conclusion that the dog had learnt something that was not innate; and if the dog had learnt to produce saliva at the mere sight of food why would he not be able to produce saliva at anything that was connected with eating? Pavlov was soon able to prove his theory, causing the dogs to produce salivary responses (conditioned responses) on hearing a bell, a metronome, a sequence of musical notes, etc., which were sounded immediately before the dogs were given food. Pavlov was able to measure the response quantitatively with the aid of an operation which made the duct of one of the salivary glands deliver the saliva outside the cheek.

When the experiment had been repeated a few times the salivary response occurred even without being followed by food. If the food was excluded too many times in succession, there would be an extinction of the response. It would, however, be restored after a day's rest. A dog could learn a lot of different patterns of behaviour through conditioned responses. For instance, he could learn to discriminate very keenly between notes of different pitch and react accordingly.

The application of this principle to the teacher-pupil situation is obvious. When pupils are indifferent to the subject-matter an attempt should be made to connect it with something that, metaphorically speaking, whets the appetite. This 'appetizer' may be anything that motivates. For instance, the chance of achieving success as a soloist encourages a piano student to practise what he might otherwise find boring.

If we turn back to the situation of the conditioned dogs, we may imagine that a dog not only salivated, wagged his tail, etc., when getting his food, but also at the sight of the keeper who used to bring him food, etc. In other words a generalization of the conditioned response had been established.

Generalization of this kind is very common in a classroom. A positive teacher creates a generalized positive atmosphere about his teaching. It might start with a rewarding word to a pupil now and then. The pupil is 'appetized' and wants more reward. His liking for reward is generalized as conditioned connection to the rewarding teacher, his tuition, and the subject-matter he teaches.

There is also a negative conditioning. A dog can be taught to avoid a certain behaviour, for instance, a light signal. Negative conditioning may also be generalized. That happens in a classroom too. A surly teacher creates an atmosphere of negative conditioning about him. It might start with a single punishment of a pupil, and if the punishment becomes an every-day occurrence there will soon be established a negatively generalized conditioning between the pupils and the teacher himself, his teaching, and his subject-matter.

Thorndike

About the same time as Pavlov's experiment, Thorndike performed his classical experiment with cats in puzzle boxes. A cat placed in a box could open the door by pressing down a lever. It learnt this by the method of *trial and error*, i.e., the cat struggled with claws and mouth at any opening or thing within the box until it happened accidentally to press the lever, and thus escape from the confinement through the open door.

In connection with these experiments Thorndike formulated his three laws of readiness, frequency, and effect. Readiness: the cat was ready to learn because of its desire for freedom. Frequency: the cat learnt through repeated trials. Effect: the positive effect of pressing the lever made the cat learn this specific behaviour, while all the other kinds of behaviour in the box were not learnt. There is a negative side of the law of effect: a negative effect is connected with learning to avoid a certain behaviour.

The practical application of this in the teacher-pupil interaction is quite obvious. The law of readiness tells us to provide opportunities of learning so arranged as to make our pupils want to learn. This readiness to learn usually exists in the children as a desire for success, a desire to prove their ability to themselves and others. The readiness, or motivation, may be reinforced by the teacher in different ways. He may present the subject-matter in an interesting way. For example, a piece of music may be more inspiring if the music teacher tells his pupils something about the composer of the piece.

The law of frequency means that a pupil must be made to practise. This, of course, is not a new fact to a music teacher, but it should be understood to work in connection with the two other laws.

The application of the law of effect is naturally reward (positive effect), and punishment (negative effect). The effect is not quite the same as 'learning result'. Having learnt to play a piano piece is the 'learning result'. Feeling satisfied with the accomplishment is the positive effect. As with the cat in the learning box, pressing the lever was the 'learning result', satisfaction at the door being opened to freedom was the positive effect.

Skinner

An experiment with a rat, which shows considerable resemblance to Thorndike's experiment, was performed by Skinner. Skinner taught a rat to press a lever in a box, rewarding ('reinforcing' in Skinner's terminology) the rat with a food pellet whenever the rat succeeded in pressing the lever. It looks very much like an application of Thorndike's law of effect. In his theory, however, Skinner laid special stress on the need for reinforcement, step by step. Skinner's theory is thus a theory of *reinforcement*. It is also called *instrumental*, or *operant*, conditioning when compared to Pavlov's dog experiment. The rat was conditioned but did not have to wait for a stimulus to occur, as was the case with Pavlov's dog, but itself *operated* an *instrument*—the lever—to produce its reward. Skinner's theory became the scientific basis for programmed learning. This method had indeed been used before but the application of Skinner's theory gave an impetus to the method.

The programmed method implies that the subject matter is split up into small steps, presented to the pupil one after the other. Each step, containing a question to be answered, a problem, or part of a problem to be solved, is immediately reinforced, i.e., the pupil is at once informed whether his response is right or wrong. The programme must be carefully tested as to degree of difficulty, so that learning can proceed without the aid of a teacher. In order to facilitate the learning and avoid cheating, learning machines of various types have been constructed. They produce the items one at a time; the pupil gives his answer, and the machine produces the reinforcement, together with the next question.

The essential point about programmed instruction, however, is not whether to use machines or books, but the special preparation of the subject-matter, the construction of the single learning steps, the rate of increasing difficulty, and the reinforcement.

The programmes may be linear or branched. A linear programme means that all students get exactly the same programme. However, each one works with his own programme and at his own speed. A branched programme guides the students to different branches of varying difficulty. A weak student is guided to a branch with exhaustive explanations and repetitions. A clever student is guided to a more difficult branch with fewer explanations and repetitions.

Programmed instruction with the use of tape recordings, concerning, for instance, elements of musical theory, including practice in listening to and classifying intervals and chords, etc., is without doubt useful in musical education.

Köhler

Köhler's well-known experiment was made with a chimpanzee. The chimpanzee, being in a cage, was offered a banana outside the cage, beyond his reach. After some futile attempts the chimpanzee stopped stretching for the banana and sat down 'thinking'. Suddenly he got 'insight' into solving the problem by joining two bamboo canes and using the lengthened tool to get the desired banana. Köhler stresses the suddenness of the insight. Something like a brainwave happens that would cause the ape to exclaim—if it could speak—"Aha, that's how to solve the problem!"

Probably some problems at school are, or could be, solved by insight. Suppose a piano teacher is asked by the pupil: "Why can't I use my thumb on the key of c sharp?" What will the teacher's answer be? Will the pupil just be snubbed or will he be given a chance of insight? The tutor could say: "Have you noticed that your fingers are of different lengths?" "Aha," the pupil would reply. "The thumb is too short to use comfortably on the black keys, so I see I must change the fingering." It is a good rule in teaching sometimes to answer a question with a question, to make the pupil use his brain to get an insight.

None of the four classical experiments or theories are to be seen as a universal way of learning. Many researchers have aimed at finding such a settlement of the question but none of the solutions can be considered as final. Some of them, the connectionists, have laid stress on the necessity of connection, association between former and new cognition. Others, the purposivists, have pointed out that hardly any learning will take place without some known or unknown purpose.

Eventually one of the later theories of Gagné may be most applicable in practical educational work. He holds that there are not more nor less than eight levels at which learning takes place, the lowest level being the level of signal-learning, i.e., the Pavlovian conditioning of a reflex type. Somewhere in the middle levels we recognize Thorndike and Skinner on levels of chaining and multiple discrimination, i.e., chains of motor and verbal associations and discriminations; whereas Köhler would be on the high levels of concept learning and problem solving. According to Gagné a higher level must have the underlying levels as prerequisite conditions of learning. For practical use, however, it will not be necessary to accept any one theory as an educational 'salvation', but the teacher should draw on conclusions from any theory to assist him in his work.

The student Edvard Grieg

Now let us look at theory put into practice. In Johanne Grieg Cederblad's biography of Edvard Grieg we read (pp. 31–33) of the fifteen-year-old Grieg's experiences at the conservatory of Leipzig.

> No doubt the dramatic, hot-tempered Edvard Grieg felt like running away from the whole business after he had had his first piano lesson. Was it to get this experience that he had been sent away from home by Ole Bull?
> Close to the piano was a stout and bald-headed man with his right forefinger under his ear didactically repeating: "Immer langsam, stark, hochheben, langsam, stark, hochheben . . ."[1]
> It was that occasion that started the bitterness that Edvard Grieg always felt towards the conservatory at Leipzig. We hear it from his lips several times. Once he writes to his Dutch friend, Julius Röntgen, complaining about his lack of technique in composition: "For this however I have not only myself to blame but above all the damned Leipzig Conservatory, where I definitely learnt nothing at all . . ."

> The one teacher who got Edvard Grieg's devotion and love was the old Moritz Hauptmann. The young man, transplanted into foreign ground, was always longing for kindness. From the moment when Hauptmann said to Edvard Grieg that they were to be good friends Grieg was willing to die for him.

[1] "Ever slow, strong, lift high, slow, strong, lift high . . ."

Charming and of tender humour is the picture that Edward Grieg gives us of his old master, who, because of his illness, gave his lessons at his home, the Thomas School, the old lodgings of Bach. He was sitting on his sofa in dressing-gown and skull-cap, spectacles on his nose, and, while the yellow-brown sap of snuff dropped from his nose down into Edvard Grieg's practice book, he made his delicate comments bearing witness to the power of his mind. The sixteen-year-old boy was composing and when Hauptmann nodded his old head and said: "Sehr schön, sehr musikalisch",[1] Edvard Grieg knew that he had made a good start on the way that is the road of the arts.

This description of Grieg's situation in Leipzig gives us a picture of two quite different teachers. The first one was strongly methodical. Apparently he applied Thorndike's law of frequency: the more practice the more skill. Surely there was also a readiness to learn present in Grieg. He must have seriously wanted to study piano when he started in Leipzig. What was missing was the positive effect (Thorndike), or reinforcement (Skinner), or appetizer (Pavlov). The teacher did not give the boy a word of encouragement or at least tell him he was right when he was. In treating Grieg as a beginner, without giving him reason, he made him feel depressed, and prepared for an atmosphere of negative conditioning, i.e., trying to avoid mistakes instead of heading for success. Nor did he give the boy the chance of insight (Köhler). The teacher had solved all the problems in using his well-tried method. Probably the method was used in the same way with all students. Having admitted them to the conservatory, the master considered them suitable for his method, rather than the method suitable for the students.

How different was the old master, Hauptmann. He prepared, from the beginning, for an atmosphere of generalized positive conditioning (Pavlov), rewarding the pupil and making friends with him (positive effect according to Thorndike, reinforcement according to Skinner). And what about his comments on Grieg's practice-book in composition? Surely Grieg—although it is not specifically stated in the biography—must have been treated on the level of concept learning and problem solving (Gagné) partly by insight (Köhler) implying also some reasoning and 'aha-experience'.

The method of experimental and control groups

The classical animal experiments have been used to illustrate theories of learning. We have seen that reward and punishment play an

---

[1] "Very beautiful, very musical."

important part in primitive learning. We will now see how reward and punishment affect learning in human experiments. One of the most well-known experiments in this field was carried out by Elisabeth Hurlock. She used the method of experimental and control groups. This method implies the use of one or several experimental groups of subjects who are exposed to certain procedures causing certain consequences. Besides the experimental groups one control group is used and this group is only exposed to what is considered a 'normal' procedure. The consequences observed in the experimental groups are then compared with the results of the control group.

In her experiment Hurlock used four different groups (Fig. 16).

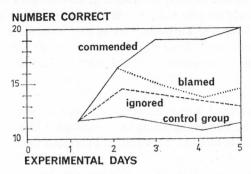

Fig. 16. Elisabeth Hurlock's experiment.

All the groups were then given the same arithmetic tests during a series of five days. The first group was commended all the time and also made progress all the time. The second group was blamed after each test. The result of this group improved to begin with, but then changed and went down. The final result, however, was some improvement in comparison with the level at the beginning. The third group was placed in the same room as the first two groups but ignored, i.e., neither commended nor blamed. This group also improved a little to begin with, but not as much as either of the first two groups. The final result was even worse than that of the blamed group. The fourth group was a control group. It was placed in a room by itself and neither commended nor blamed. This group did not change its results very much from one test to the other, and the final result was neither improvement nor regression.

The experiment shows that credit and blame may both be used, and that credit should be used the more frequently.

An interesting experiment of rather similar design has been carried out by Ingvar Johannesson and, on the whole, with the same result. However, one detail of special interest must be mentioned. Johannesson found that credit and blame were of the utmost effect in mechanical counting in arithmetic but rather small in problem solving. The probable explanation is that the solution of a problem *per se* involves a high degree of automatic reinforcement, whereas the mechanical counting, as a matter of routine, is felt to be monotonous and boring. That is why the teacher's encouragement is more necessary in the latter case.

Johannesson's experiment again calls to mind Grieg's two teachers. The first teacher tried to make his pupil acquire a good technique of touch on the keys by routine practice. This was no doubt monotonous and boring to the pupil who obviously, according to Johannesson's statement, should have had an extra amount of encouragement in that kind of training, which—as we have seen—he did not get. In his work on composition, however, he did well, not only because the teacher Hauptmann gave him credit, but also because this kind of work, like the solution of problems, must have had a great deal of self-reinforcement.

Learning curves

Numerous experiments on learning like that of Hurlock have been so designed that the results can be registered as curves of learning and of

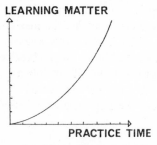

Fig. 17. Learning curve showing positive acceleration. The improvement is slow at the beginning but becomes more rapid as the subject becomes more proficient.

Fig. 18. Learning curve showing negative acceleration. The improvement is rapid at the start and then begins to slow down.

59

forgetting. The first experiments of this kind were performed by Ebbinghaus, at the end of the nineteenth century. He used nonsense syllables such as *meev, jish, glet, fape, daux,* and the like. The idea of the use of nonsense material was that such syllables provided a large quantity of material of fairly uniform difficulty. Because they were meaningless they could not form any meaningful associations between themselves. As a measure for constructing a learning curve, one could, for instance, see how many syllables the subjects memorized within certain time limits: how many in five minutes, 10 minutes, 15 minutes, etc. In the same way one could have a curve of forgetting, if one made the subjects reproduce as many syllables as possible after certain time limits had expired.

In fact there are no theoretical limits to the possible variations of learning curves; but some are of a rather general type, and some discussion of them may be of practical use in teaching. Thus the following types should be discussed: positively and negatively accelerated curves, s-curves, and plateau-curves.

Positive acceleration

The condition of a learning curve becoming positively accelerated is that the subject matter is new to the pupil. When the curve is cut short at the top the learning has not reached its maximum. If the curve has this form in practical tuition it means that we must encourage the pupil at the start in order to make him go on. To break off a practice may be necessary for various reasons, but if possible a successful practice of, for instance, a piano piece, should be resumed on another occasion and not be broken off until the pupil has experienced the full benefit of success (Fig. 17).

Negative acceleration

A negatively accelerated curve occurs if the pupil has former knowledge or skill in the subject matter. The learning is then built on this previously acquired knowledge or skill and is very rapid at the start. The curve starts steeply. Eventually, as the student reaches his maximal learning capacity, the acceleration decreases. Near the border of maximum, the progress per unit of time is very small. A student who is near his maximum thus must make an extra great effort to reach the very top of his ability, and at this stage he may need much encouragement from the teacher. It may, for instance, be the last preparation for a début or an examination (Fig. 18).

The S-curve

The positively and negatively accelerated curves, put together, constitute what is called an S-curve; this represents the complete learning of uncomplicated subject matter (Fig. 19).

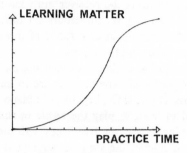

Fig. 19. The S-curve.

The plateau

The occurrence of plateaux in learning curves were first noticed by Bryan and Harter in the eighteen-nineties when observing the learning of morse code. After about fourteen weeks of practice (see Fig. 20) they found a period of standstill, a plateau, in the skill of receiving. After about another ten weeks, however, a new period of rapid progress started.

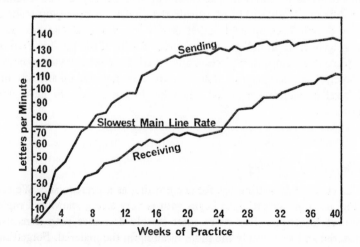

Fig. 20. (From Bryan & Harter, 1897.) Learning curves of one student of telegraphy, tested once a week in sending and receiving connected messages.

The general conclusion to be drawn from the existence of these plateaux is that there is a latent learning going on during the period of the plateau. The latent learning in the case of receiving telegraphy should be the perception of the letters and words as connected discourse, instead of mere disconnected letters or words. In other words: during the period of latent learning the receiver must have time to spell out any word that happens to give him trouble. Until his vocabulary of 'auditory-click' words reaches nearly 100% of those in common use, his receiving rate will stay on the plateau.

The general conclusion is that a plateau occurs when the subject matter consists of part-achievements that are to be coordinated to a whole-achievement. For instance, beginners in piano according to older methods first had to learn to play the treble of the piano with both hands before learning to play the bass notes with the left hand. When after some weeks of practice the left hand attempted bass notes instead of treble notes there occurred a plateau before the new part-achievement had been coordinated to the whole-achievement of treble and bass put together. Modern methods avoid this plateau by starting with the thumbs of the two hands on the middle C. Bass and treble are then developed symmetrically and simultaneously with the left and right hands respectively.

As has been said the reason for a plateau is involved in the nature of the subject matter or skill. However, there may be many other different causes. For instance the cause may be that the teacher has forced his tuition too fast. The remedy, in this case, is repetition and a more careful preparation. The cause of a plateau may also be troubles of different kinds within or outside the studies. A grown-up student may benefit from an explanation of the occurrence of plateaux. Encouragement is an indispensable source of help. If the pupil is tired of a piece of music, easier pieces could be tried, or other styles of music chosen. One must see to it that the pupil does not give up and lose his self-reliance during a period when he does not seem to make any progress.

The curve of forgetting

The curve of forgetting has former learning as a prerequisite. We see (Fig. 21) that forgetting to begin with is very steep, showing a rapid rate of forgetting. The curve most steeply decreases with nonsense material and less steeply the more meaningful the material. Forgetting should if possible be counteracted with repetition while retention is still above the threshold of recall, i.e., can be immediately recalled.

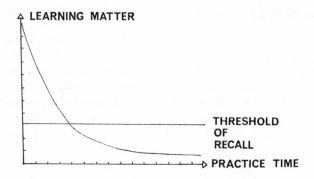

Fig. 21. Curve of forgetting. The curve shows how the retention of what has been learnt rapidly decreases as soon as the learning ceases.

Overlearning

Overlearning may be explained as repetition 'in advance'. The learning, practice, etc., is not made only to the level of the threshold of recall, but beyond. If the practice is stopped at the level of recall, the curve of forgetting will at once fall beneath the threshold. Recall may not be possible after a very short interval of time but a few extra repetitions, some extra practice above the level of immediate recall, will raise the initial level of the curve of forgetting, and a longer interval of time may pass before retention falls below the threshold of recall. Thus the longer we want to remember the learned function the more intensive should be the overlearning. However, in the practical learning situation one must remember that additional factors are of importance. Fatigue, lack of motivation, etc., may spoil overlearning. In such a case, of course, repetition or practice had better wait until the pupil has had a period of rest, or indulged in other occupations.

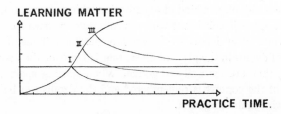

Fig. 22. Different degrees of overlearning. Curve I shows a function practised to the level of immediate recall. Curve II shows some overlearning, and the result of learning lasting for a longer time above the threshold of recall. Curve III shows overlearning nearer to maximum of ability and retention; and the curve does not fall below the level of recall.

The piece left to mature

It may happen that the practice of a piece of music will get stuck through faulty fingering or for some other reason. It may then be of advantage to stop practising the piece for some time. Starting afresh on the piece one may find the faults miraculously gone. The reason for this phenomenon, called 'reminiscense', may be the differentiation of forgetting (McGeoch), i.e., one remembers what is correctly memorized but forgets the incorrectly (less well established) memorized matter (Fig. 23).

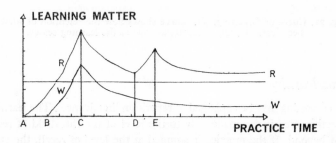

Fig. 23. The curves show what happens in respect of reminiscence when some passage of a piece of music is left to mature. The practice starts at A, the R-curve showing what is correctly learnt. At B an error, faulty fingering for instance, is involved. What is learnt wrongly is represented by the W-curve. At C the practice ceases and both curves are showing decreasing retention. The R-curve, however, remains above the level of immediate recall while the W-curve rapidly falls beneath the threshold. At D a repetition occurs. The repetition has no effect on the W-curve which remains below the level of immediate recall. The pupil is lucky not to remember his faulty fingering. On the other hand the R-curve rises from point D to point E and when practice again ceases the correctly learned passages stay as definitely established above the level of recall.

Another explanation may be that an unpleasant memory anyway is more easily forgotten than a pleasant one.

There is also often a kind of organization taking place in remembered material. What is consistent with the meaning or structure is remembered while lesser details are forgotten or modified. Thus, if the errors consist of details in the piece of music that fall outside the main musical context, they are naturally forgotten. When starting again the broad outline of the context is remembered and the details can be practised afresh with faults forgotten.

Which of the explanations is applicable in a special case is of no importance in practice. What is essential is that there *are* one or more explanations that make the teacher and his pupil believe in the facts of reminiscence as an aid to practice.

Positive transfer

When practising music, instrumental or vocal, the possibilities of positive transfer should be considered. The meaning of positive transfer is that details or techniques learned and used in one field may be transferred to, and used in, another field. For instance, having learned to play a recorder it will be easier, because of positive transfer, to start with a transverse flute. The notes are the same on both instruments. Training to play in tune may also be of the same value with both instruments. Thus it may be of advantage, in instrumental schools, private or municipal, to start all tuition of the beginners with a period of group tuition on the recorder or some other instrument suitable for group tuition. The positive transfer will probably be considerable enough to compensate for some of the loss of time for the single talented pupil who would have preferred to learn to play his final instrument from the beginning. The advantages of an economic and organizational nature are also apparent when group teaching is used in the elements of music with the aid of recorders, tuned percussion instruments, and the like.

Positive transfer may also be used when practising a piece of music. One must look through the piece and discover similarities—not only where there is actual recapitulation but also similarities in passages and details such as phrasing, fingering, etc. Often there are similarities, for instance in melody and harmony in different parts of the piece, that could be discovered, resulting in easier learning and other effects of positive transfer.

Negative transfer

The effects of negative transfer are often called associative *inhibitions*. These can be either *proactive* or *retroactive*.

The proactive inhibition implies that the learning of new subject-matter is rendered more difficult because of the former learning of rather similar matter. The associations of similarity are the stronger the more similar the materials. For instance, the knowledge of the English word 'flesh' may be an obstacle in learning of the German word 'Fleisch' when studying the German language. The similarity of spelling and pronunciation will be an obstacle to learning the slight difference of meaning, as the German word 'Fleisch' should be translated by the English word 'meat', and not 'flesh'.

The retroactive inhibition means that the retention of former learned matter is destroyed by a later learned, rather similar, matter. For instance, the last part of the Swedish song *Saint Lucia* is recapitulated with a change of only two notes (see Fig. 24). Of the two phrases the last one is remembered and the first one forgotten, so what one might remember, because of retroactive inhibition, is only the last version sung twice.

Fig. 24. *Saint Lucia.* The last two phrases are confused because of retroactive inhibition on the four marked notes. The last phrase is sung twice, and the penultimate phrase is left out. (The song is the most common of the many songs used in Sweden in connection with the Lucia Day celebrations. The tune is, however, not Swedish but Neapolitan. Instead of translating one of the many variants of Swedish texts the author has found it easier to compose his own version in English.)

When practising songs or other pieces of music it is essential to try to avoid negative transfer. It is wise to observe—before practice—all kinds of similarities, both technical and musical. Are the similarities quite identical? If not, where are the small differences, and how can errors be avoided in practising these? Can negative transfer be avoided?

The role of associative inhibitions is very great.[1] Carelessness with fingering may be the most common cause of associative inhibitions when practising music. What happens is that two or more competing fingerings are associated in the memory with, for example, a single

---

[1] It should be observed that inhibition in this case has nothing to do with inhibition in the psycho-analytical sense.

melodic phrase. When speeding up the tempo the different fingerings previously used will compete with each other and spoil the technique. "Both the thumb and the forefinger want to play the note D. Now, which one will it be?" There is only one way to avoid inhibitions of careless fingerings. That is to practise very carefully and concentrate on one single fingering from the very beginning. Some overlearning is also advisable at this slow tempo. Music teachers often hold that "speed comes by itself", and there is surely a great deal of truth in this, provided that one habit of movement—and only one—is first established.

Massed and distributed practice

The disposition of learning time and learning material is of considerable importance. In organizing learning time one may choose between *massed* and *distributed practice*. *Whole* and *part method* are the respective terms used about the disposition of learning material.

As to the disposition of the *time* of learning, statistics provide un-ambiguous and clear evidence in favour of distributed practice. It is thus better to practise a piece of music for five half-hours, distributed over five different days, than to practise all the five half-hours on one day without a break. Mere risk of fatigue is reason enough, but also what has been said earlier about the method of leaving a piece to mature (reminiscence) is relevant. What is eventually learnt inaccurately will have time to be forgotten if learning time is distributed. Thus, if music is to be learned for a musical examination or a public perform-ance, practice must start in good time to make possible a suitable distribution of the practice-time. If such a scheme is carried out less time will be needed, and the performance will be better. Of course, the same is applicable to choir work or any other kind of learning as, for instance, history or theory of music.

Whole and part method

When we consider the disposition of subject matter the choice between whole and part method is not easy, as the statistical evidence is not unambiguous. So rather than choose one of the methods it is better to make use of both. It is advisable first to make a survey of the subject (whole method) and then go to the details (part method). When the details are clear they may be put together within the framework of knowledge that has been built on the first survey. The method may be considered to be one of 'synthesis—analysis—synthesis'.

How to study a textbook

As an illustration of the foregoing we now show what a page of a textbook will be like after being used by a student. One can see in the marginal notes of the student that he has used the synthesis—analysis—synthesis method. The first survey corresponds to the use of the capital letters *A*, *B*, and *C* in the margin as well as the *double-underlined words* in the text. Then he has made an analysis of details, marked with *numbers* and *single-underlined words*, and, sometimes, where there has been a need for splitting up a detail from different points of view, he has used *small letters*. Having made this synthesis (*A*, *B*, *C*), the analysis of details, and, in addition, a summary (final synthesis) with the main points, he will feel fully acquainted with the subject-matter when returning for revision before a final examination. He will then, without too much effort, manage to memorize the main points and the detail is more likely to be recalled in association with these main points.

A Synthesis — If starting with a textbook for an examination it is advisable at first to make [A]/a general survey of the book, i.e., have a look at the [1]/table of contents, read the [2]/preface, and take [3]/a rapid glance at the book as a whole, especially the [4]/headings and the like.

B Analysis — Then one may turn to the [B]/single chapters for a closer study. Essential sentences are [1]/underlined. The matter is arranged into [2]/classifications, divisions, and subdivisions *with* with the aid of [a]numbers (viewpoints no. 1, no. 2, no. 3, *self-* etc.) and [b]/marginal notes. An important thing is the *control* [3]/self-control. One must [a]/not read too extended parts before testing oneself with a self-control, i.e., reviewing the section in one's own words. [b]/Single sentences and rules, important years and terms may have to be memorized. Generally one must feel [c]/free from the wordings of the book. [4a]/Reading aloud may assist concentration. On the other hand, [b]/reading silently is usually quicker. The gain in time, together with the fact that most people are able to concentrate just as well when reading silently, makes it [c]/advisable to read silently in most cases.

After the detailed analysis of the single chapters it is
C Synthesis advisable to make ^{c/}summaries of ^{1/}the chapters followed by a ^{2/}repeated review of the book as a whole. This may be necessary and rather like going away some distance from the trees in order to be able to see the whole wood.

How to study a piece of music

The method of synthesis—analysis—synthesis is recommended in studying a piece of music. At the first survey and during the following analysis of details, it is advisable to make a habit of looking for similarities and dissimilarities, in order to be able to utilize positive transfer and avoid associative inhibitions. The smaller dissimilarities that may be discovered should at once be marked in some way with pen or pencil in order to avoid inhibitions, for instance melodic or rhythmic sequences. To the stage of detailed analysis also belongs the testing and making of comfortable fingerings that must then be strictly obeyed in the ensuing practice in order to avoid competing motor habits of different fingerings. Competing habits must, of course, be avoided in cases other than fingering such as, for instance, phrasing. Other examples are bowing in stringed instruments, and breathing in song and wind instruments. Why not sometimes use a red pencil to make a warning sign (see page 25 concerning figure-ground-relation)? A singer or a violinist may be afraid of singing or playing a note slightly below correct pitch. An arrow pointing upwards before the note will call the attention to this. Firstly, the use of the pencil has the advantage of some overlearning when making the mark in the score. Secondly, the mark, as constituted by the arrow, tells one the specified kind of fault that is to be avoided. *Never let a fault happen without at once making a correction, if you do not want it to recur !*

Having made this detailed analysis the practice will start, and during the practice do not forget what has been said about the great advantages of distributed practice, and the necessity of starting the practice in good time before the performance. As with the study of textbooks it is also advisable to use a method of 'self-control'. This should not always be done at the instrument. It is useful to play music as well as sing songs in the imagination. Harmonies, tunes, fingering, bowing, nuances, everything about the music may be imagined, sitting in an armchair with eyes shut to increase the concentration of inner listening and imagination of technique.

Study habits, hygiene

We have seen the risk of careless fingering and other undesirable habits hindering technique. While such habits are to be avoided, there are, on the other hand, good habits to be acquired. It is, for instance, a good form of discipline always to *practise at the same time of day, in the same place and on the same days of the week*. If a timetable is thus established and made a habit, the habit in itself will eventually become a strong aid in keeping the studies going.

In connection with questions of learning and technique of study something also should be said about hygiene. One thing to consider is the *lighting*. This should be controlled. Bad lighting at the piano, or at the music stands of other instrumentalists, is unfortunately not particularly unusual. Many young beginners suffer from the disadvantage of this, and it is not altogether uncommon even with grown-ups. Note reading really is a strain on the eyes and calls for special concentration. An eye specialist should be consulted in cases of special fatigue in connection with note reading as special note reading spectacles may be needed. The *distance between the music, the keys, and the eyes* is not always the same as between the eyes and the book that is being read, nor is it always the same between the music stand at home and the music stand of the teacher's grand piano. This may be of considerable disadvantage to young beginners, as the eyes are sometimes fixed upon the keys, sometimes upon the score. Also the *height of the piano-stool* must be considered. For young children an extra foot-stool may be needed. Finally, one must stress the importance of fresh air in the room, and the importance of regular breaks during practice. Perhaps it should also be said that a student of music should not neglect the need for rest, and, like other students, should generally sleep at least eight hours a night.

Developmental Psychology and Learning

7

Much work has been done to analyse and understand development and growth in various respects which naturally have a bearing on learning. Charlotte and Karl Bühler, Jean Piaget, and Arnold Gesell are some of the best-known scientists in the world.

The usual way to introduce developmental psychology to the reader is to discuss certain periods regarding motor, linguistic, adaptive, social, emotional, and intellectual development. Scientists differ, however, quite often both as to definition and stages of development, maturity, and growth. As far as musical development is concerned we can hardly divide it into periods until our knowledge is more satisfactory for such a purpose.

The ages mentioned in the following sub-headings only serve to arrange the subject-matter in a sensible way.

Between five and eight

An infant teacher usually has her first contact with pupils when they are between five and six. In Sweden children start school at the age of seven, in the USA at six and in England at five. The instrumental teacher usually meets the pupils at a later age.

The early school attendance tells us something of what can be expected from the children at that age. The ability to coordinate eye and hand must be sufficiently developed to make it possible to learn to write. Individual differences, of course, occur frequently. In instrumental music you need coordination, not only of eye and hand but also of ear, and that naturally does not facilitate instrumental learning. Moreover the hands are too small for some instruments. For example, a child of seven cannot avoid leaks when playing the soprano-recorder, while a child of eight will have no difficulty. Octaves have been taken away from most of the piano-music for children. The use of chords in music for infant-beginners should not necessarily be avoided but the chords should have a small range and must be arranged to suit hands that are weak because the ossification is not yet completed. The learning of musical instruments should not be postponed to a later age because the hands are small and weak, but the teacher must be moderate in his demands on the pupil's motor skill. Most of the great virtuosi have started to learn playing an instrument at a very early age. They and their masters often point out the importance of starting while the hands are still slightly cartilaginous and supple and are able to grow into the special posture that, for example, is required by a violin. The violin used at first must, of course, be of a small size. As regards the great virtuosi, who have started at an exceptionally early age, they have not only been musically talented but also physically and intellectually precocious.

In this connection may be mentioned an interesting observation by the Dutchman, Camille Jacobs, concerning beginners of the violin, between the ages of $11\frac{1}{2}$ and 13. Jacobs compared two groups of beginners. One group consisted of ten pupils with trained musical hearing, the other of ten pupils with untrained musical hearing. The investigator does not mention in what way the musically trained had been trained. However, the comparison between the two groups showed that the group with trained musical hearing made more mistakes than the untrained group. Jacobs draws the conclusion that the musically trained pupils were highly disturbed whenever they played out of tune. Because of this their attention was not focused upon the means by which the notes were to be produced, so they did not make the right finger-movements. The musically untrained were easier to correct, because it was easier to make them respond to comments on the pattern of movement.

Without generalizing too much from this experiment with small groups one can draw the conclusion that it would be wise if teachers of wind- and string-instruments allowed beginners to play a little out of tune. Instead of correct pitch one should ask for a beautiful sound-quality and see to it that the short music pieces for beginners are played straight through in a recognizable way. Eventually one can demand more correct intonation as the musculature is trained enough to be the obedient servant of the musical ear.

The child as animist

It is very important to know that the child at this stage of development has an animistic[1] disposition, i.e., they animate dead, as well as live, things in their environment. For a child the border-line between imagination and reality is indistinct. A child's lie is not always a real lie but may be sheer fantasy or self-suggestion. The chair 'hurts itself', when it is overturned. Animals think and speak like human beings but in their own special way. At this age of imagination children's games are

[1] animistic from latin *anima* = soul.

also games of imagination. They pretend to be animals, or characters from fairy-tales, or grown-ups. That is why the traditional nursery rhymes and similar songs, which are about animals and various figures out of fairy-tales, or admit of dramatizing and imitation from the world of grown-ups, have had, and still have, such success.

The music teacher should not only in his choice of songs satisfy the children's animistic disposition, but also in his choice of method. There are many situations in which this is worthwhile. He can, for example, call quavers running notes and crochets walking notes. The names of notes can be personified: Cecily's note, David's note, Eric's note, etc. The experience of the key-note can be a short little tale about the birds who find their way home to their nest, which is the last note of the melody. The animistic fairy age is, of course, the golden age for romantic programme music. The tutors of different instruments as a rule take this into account when giving romantic titles to the pieces of practice. The teacher should not neglect to make the most of the possibilities and turn the pieces into artistic interpretations. Be sure to take these headings seriously, when you are teaching children of this age. Use your imagination and dramatize. Here the objection can be made that the more musically talented the children are, the less they need non-musical inspiration. Even if such objections are valid, one must always remember that children are children. They are not musical whether animistic or not. But they are animistic whether musical or not.

The child in the world of dimensions

What has been said above is also true of the world of dimensions. The author, who left one of his homes of childhood at the age of eight, received something of a shock thirty years later when he returned to the same place. The enormous building that he remembered from his childhood proved to be quite an ordinary house.

What adults look upon as trifles, children look upon as being big and important. This is also true of what we teach. When a child learns a new note, a new fingering, a new chord on his instrument, it is to him a big step forward. The teacher should therefore treat such parts of a curriculum with great care, even if to him they are only details. Things that appear important to the child also tend to cause strong emotional reactions. It has been said that the child's emotional reactions are not as distinct and diversified as the adult's. This may be both true and false. The child gets extremely happy or unhappy more easily than the adult and does not have the same ability to pretend. But why do we always compare children with adults? How much are we as adults able to know about, or sympathize with, children's petty troubles or causes of rejoicing ? Probably not very much. How could grown-ups emotionally experience little things as acutely as children do because they themselves are so small ? Let us take the children's emotional life seriously and try to look at it with the children's own dimensions. If the child—having just achieved a five-note-range on the key-board—ascends a fifth with the melody, why shouldn't he imagine a little mountaineering and feel a little triumphant about it ? As teachers we must accept a case like that and rid ourselves of the methodological and artistic obstacles inherent in the statement that children do not have a diversified emotional life.

The monotone problem and the vocal pitch range

Of great importance in class-teaching is knowledge of children's vocal pitch range and the development of the musical ear. Some investigations in the field have been made but the conditions of the children's performance have been rather different and cannot be compared on equal terms. Before stating a certain pitch range for a certain age the question of whether to take the monotones into account ought to be resolved. The genuine monotone only produces one 'note', suiting his own comfortable pitch, and sticks to that single note when he 'sings' a melody.[1] If monotones are taken into consideration when statistics are made, the pitch range for the average child of a certain age will be narrower than if they are disregarded.

In addition to the genuine monotones there are many pupils who are called monotones but in fact are not real monotones. They sing off pitch in different ways, sometimes because their voices cannot physically reach the highest or lowest notes in the song, sometimes because of lack of co-operation between mind and vocal cords, although they do not lack musical ear. Then there are, of course, those who sing more or less out of tune because of deficiency of musical ear. Some of the latter category are able to stick to the right pitch, when they have the aid of the melody from a musical instrument. Some can follow the tune all right while the melody keeps to one key, but have difficulty when transitions occur. Some pupils sing just a little too high or too low more or less all the time. All these different degrees of ability to keep in tune—from perfectly correct singing to real monotone singing—must be taken into consideration when the vocal pitch range at different

---

[1] The definition may be considered a little too theoretic and tied up to the word-meaning of monotone. One of the recent investigators in the field, David Joyner, says of the most genuine monotones of his experimental group that they "had no comfortable range at all, seeming to experience difficulty in producing tone on any pitch."

ages is investigated. The common method used is to make the subject imitate a scale or a melody transposed to different levels.

As has been said before, the different investigations cannot be compared on equal terms but that does not prevent us from drawing some general conclusions for practical use. Firstly, it is clear that the average voice range increases with age. Secondly, proper training is reported to have an increasing effect on the voice range. Thirdly, the songs in children's songbooks are by some investigators reported to have pitch levels that are too high for many children. Fourthly, the percentage of monotones—both real and non-real—is reported to diminish proportionately to increasing voice range with growing age and as a result of training.

According to the above-mentioned conclusions songs in class-singing should be presented in different pitch levels and teachers should see to it that children with a low level pitch range are also provided for. There are two ways to do this. Either publishers of songbooks should include transposed arrangements for different pitch levels or one should demand of the teachers the ability to transpose simple tunes.

Many teachers, who are good voice trainers, are able to show classes of children with special ability to sing high notes with superior quality of voice. This is, however, the result of continuous voice training and is no contradiction of the fact that a successful voice teacher always has to start on the pupil's own level, which means with songs of rather a limited voice range.

What has been said also has a bearing on the marking in music. If marking is used at all, it should be done with extra care in the first school-ages. Especially the use of the lowest marks should be restricted. Obviously a low mark given early because of untuneful singing very easily gives both the child and the parents the impression that continued participation in song and instrumental tuition would be pointless. In most cases this is an inadequate conclusion, since, after all, there *is* a development of both pitch range and musical ear. If the marking-scale on the whole is kept relatively high, the absence of the lowest mark does not necessarily imply any injustice to the clever pupils either.

Furthermore—in order not to overemphasize singing ability—other musical activities such as the playing of rhythm-instruments, and ability in music appreciation and musical movement should be considered when marking music ability.

A developmental pattern of child song

A widespread opinion is that the interval of the falling minor third is a very appropriate means for starting voice training especially with problem singers, i.e., those monotones who react in a positive way to training. The reason for this is that this interval is considered to be at the origin of the awakening of the sense of pitch in hearing. This early development of the sense of pitch may have an historical parallel. According to a German theory (Stumpf) the falling third developed in emergency when the primitive man had to call to somebody from a distance. Less theoretical and more topical are the observations on children's *spontaneous* formation of melodic configurations, where the falling minor third is shown to have a frequent occurrence. The same observation can be made about a lot of children's most popular songs.

From these theories and observations there has emerged a pattern of development considered to be typical of children's spontaneous singing. The first stage in this development is the falling third with a range of three notes. In the second stage a major second is added above the minor third. The third stage is a configuration within the range of six notes. This configuration may also be considered a model of a pentatonic system if you just insert one note between the two lowest in the model (see Fig. 25).

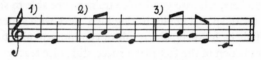

Fig. 25. Stages in the development of children's spontaneous melodic configurations.

This pattern of development can hardly be said to have enough conclusive scientific proof to form the basis of a universal method. However, being plausible it has had a great influence on methods of music tuition. An example of this is the system of the German Carl Orff, published in his *Schulwerk* (*Music for Children*).

Some investigation has been done concerning the ear for hearing simultaneous notes and the logic of harmony. It shows that children up to a certain stage in maturation of the musical mind are rather indifferent to the accompaniment of a melody. In this connection it is hardly possible to fix an average age but ages between six and nine years are mentioned by different investigators.

Teachers using tonic sol-fa claim that at a very early stage they successfully use the leading seventh note of the scale to train children to find the key-note. This implies that children trained in tonic sol-fa are supported quite early by the latent harmonic logic involved in a cadence. On the other hand, Orff's *Music for Children* dwells on harmonically neutral ostinato parts, pentatonic chord-configurations, and parallel triads, before introducing the succession of dominant and tonic chords.

Whatever the conclusion drawn from the methods of music teachers one should bear in mind that young children probably do not experience melody in the same way as grown-ups. Text and melody belong together in a more inseparable way, while accompanying harmony either tonal or pentatonic in the beginning has the character of a diffuse, uninteresting background.

To sum up, a teacher working with children between five and eight should make use of their animistic view. This should be taken advantage of when notes and measures, crotchets and other elements are introduced. It should also, of course, be considered when choosing the texts of children's songs. The melodies of the songs should have a limited range. Accompaniment should be quite simple and not include intricate harmony and transitions. The teacher should not force a pitch on his pupils, but should be able to transpose songs upwards or downwards to a comfortable pitch or pick out songs that are arranged in a comfortable pitch. In order to satisfy different pupils it can be convenient to divide a class into different groups according to voice range or musical ability or because of a desirability to give them different musical activities. The lowest marking—if marking is used—should be restricted in order not to discourage pupils from tuition who—in spite of bad qualities at this early age—may later develop a musical activity.

Between eight and puberty

The development of children between eight and puberty has a more 'realistic' tendency than that of children at an earlier age. It is more 'realistic' to play cops and robbers, cricket, or ice-hockey than mothers and fathers, keeping a sweet shop, or pretending to be a fox hunting a hare. It is still natural for children to look upon grown-ups as authorities. A teacher may misinterpret this and believe he is working on the children's wavelength. Some information on what children really like at this age can be gathered from what they spontaneously read. Considering this Charlotte Bühler described this age as the 'Robinson Crusoe age'.

Musically this is an advantageous age to work with, both instrumentally and in class-singing. The children have acquired the ability to read and write and do simple arithmetic and the teacher can use written instructions and practice books. Simple written tests can be given. The method of tuition can be given a straightforward character. The hands have grown. The muscles engaged in the playing of instruments are more developed than before. It becomes more essential for the teacher to adapt his tuition to the musical ability of the individual pupil than to consider ossification of bones or animistic viewpoints.

Working in class-singing the teacher is fortunate to find the monotones eventually reduced in number. Many instrumental tutors find eight the most suitable age for pupils to start playing an instrument, and certainly never recommended an age later than nine.

Puberty

Puberty has its special problems. There is often in the individual a disharmony caused by incongruity of sexual, social, and intellectual maturity, which goes together with the general disagreements between the older and younger generations. Some investigators hold that the difficulties of puberty have been exaggerated, others that they are still underestimated. For the music teacher it is of special interest to consider what characterizes the emotional life, the sets, and the popular music of this age.

The emotional life is considered to be very unstable, changing quickly between dark and light moments like a cloudy sky, and the possibility of some sort of artistic self-expression is in the circumstances a great adventure. So the teacher should give the pupils an opportunity to create their own music or occupy themselves with music and musical material in a creative way. If, at earlier stages, the pupils have been given appropriate instrumental or class-music tuition, they already have the necessary tools for the musical 'handicraft'. It will now be possible to encourage their own experiments in the musical workshop with tunes and rhythms of their own. Sound-laboratory work of concrete and electronic type is another possible area of creativity. The results of such work may be welcome contributions to a school-play as background music (see footnote on page 37).

The sets that are often formed among adolescents belong to the age, but sometimes develop into asocial gangs. School should do its best, however, to encourage the formation of sets with sound occupations. Thus tuition in groups and ensemble-playing should be encouraged during the school years in the hope that pupils who are accustomed to this kind of occupation will go on with it after school.

Young people's favourite music—pop music—is very much in keeping with prevalent dance-music, film-music, and other popular and commercial sounds. There develops very easily a wide gap between the music they hear at school and the music they consider their own and for this reason music teachers in schools and elsewhere should do their best to bridge the gap and try to understand young people's music. Otherwise teachers of classical music will risk failure in their educational efforts as they will make young people discard their teacher's music in favour of their own. From the music teacher's point of view there is no doubt that it is both wise and correct to consider the age of puberty as a certain musical stage, which has to be passed through. Many young people during puberty suddenly find themselves interested in music for the first time in their lives. This interest should be encouraged and developed by their music teachers.

As a summary one could say that puberty is the age at which the result of music education during earlier years manifests itself. If a solid basis of musical knowledge and practical attainments has been established early, diligent creative work in music is now possible. The music teacher has great opportunities to help pupils find artistic expression in their emotional lives. Finally the music teacher will also be able to do a lot to guide young people into groups with others with whom they can share a sound musical occupation in their leisure time. This contribution to spare time occupation appears to be of special value in the light of the juvenile delinquency problem that often arises where youth has not been able to solve its spare time problems.

Longitudinal and transversal method

In genetic psychology there are two methods of research, the *longitudinal* and the *transversal*. Longitudinal research means following one subject, or group of subjects, during a certain period of time. The American, Arnold Gesell, is famous for his research concerning the development of children from birth to sixteen years using this method. In order to be able to study the children without their being aware of it, he placed them behind a one-way-screen, i.e., in a room with glass of the kind through which the spectator can see the children, but the children cannot see the spectator.

If you want to save time, you can use the transversal method, i.e., make research on several ages at the same time, in which case instead of one group you need as many groups as the ages to be investigated.

An investigation of the school age

In a combination of transversal and longitudinal studies of children between the ages of six and twelve, consisting of about six thousand individual testings, the American, Robert Petzold, made certain investigations into musical development. He found musical development to be strikingly fast between six and seven but slower thereafter, and for this reason emphasizes the importance of good tuition during the early school years. The ages six to seven are not only interesting as far as melodic ability is concerned but also with regard to harmony. Petzold recommends a simple accompaniment of triads, but points out that more complicated harmonies do not support the learning of melodies.

Simple rhythmic patterns can be mastered by eight-year-olds, but keeping to an unchanged tempo is more difficult for them. Children between six and seven years of age have especial difficulty with slow tempos such as those with a pulse of as few as sixty beats per minute (M.M. = 60). At the age of eight about 85% of the children in Petzold's investigation had a full voice control and could sing correctly in tune, while approximately 8% of the 'problem singers' remained problem singers as long as the investigation lasted, i.e., until the age of twelve. Sex differences apparently favoured the girls in the melodic tests, but not in tests of harmony and rhythm. Petzold believes that differences—when they occur—are more a question of attitude to singing than real inability. His practical conclusion is that greater attention should be given to the non-musical differences between boys and girls, when choosing music and songs and in planning music education on the whole.

The Sequence of Musical Development and Learning

8

As we have seen in the foregoing chapter there is a certain sequence in the development of a child's abilities parallel to the stages of maturation. That is to say, for example, that a child's abilities to sit, or crawl, or walk are parallel to stages of development and maturation of the nervous system, skeleton, and muscles.

If the sequence of musical development were as well known it would certainly be appropriate to adjust any method of musical tuition to this sequence. As an example we may refer to the stages of development of children's spontaneous melodic configurations (see Fig. 25, page 76). Another example is Petzold's statement that children of six to seven years of age experience difficulty in keeping an unchanged slow tempo (page 80). Clearly it is an urgent task for future research to investigate as thoroughly as possible the musical development of children in order to be able to describe a complete sequence as a basic background for the foundations of method in musical tuition.

The sequence of musical development that eventually will be revealed as research proceeds in the field will, however, not be the source of the solution to the whole problem of method in music education. It may, for instance, help us to decide, like Petzold, that it is better to start teaching children to use crotchets and quavers in a rather rapid tempo than to start with minims, semibreves, and a slow tempo, but knowledge of the sequence of musical development will not help us to decide—when teaching crotchets and quavers—*how* to go about it, e.g., using rhythm syllables (taa, taatai), or not.

Psychological science may be able to tell us that the immediate memory span at a certain age has a certain average range and is shorter for atonal melodies than for tonal. But the consequence for teaching will not be a preference for tonal or atonal music but an inclination to use melodies with shorter phrases and more repetition when introducing atonal melodies.

A good reason for considering the sequence of child development with reference to musical method is that it may be of help when constructing *educational objectives* for a certain age. If we know, for instance, that the voice range has an average span of a sixth for a certain age we should reasonably take that into consideration when choosing songs for a class of that age.

One should, furthermore, pay more attention to the construction of educational objectives than is usually paid in music education. What is actually meant, for instance, when a curriculum says that the aim should be to give the students "some knowledge of modern music"? Does this mean using one hour or seven hours of teaching on the subject? Does it mean music from 1900 up till now, or does it mean music from 1950 up till now? Does it mean listening to records, or a performance of songs, or taking a written examination? Would it not be of considerable advantage for the teacher as well as the students if objectives could be more clearly specified? Another wording of this objective for students of musicology could for instance be: "The students are—after eight hours of instruction and listening—expected to be able to tell whether an opus like Stockhausen's *Gesang der Jünglinge* (*Song of the Disciples*) is concrete music, electronic, electrophonic, atonal, impressionistic, or expressionistic. They should be able to define these words and name five composers and at least one of the most typical works of each, which they have heard wholly or in extracts. When listening to an extract from any of these works, the students should be able to recognize to which work it belongs as well as to name its composer." The character of such a description of an objective is not only that it is more specific as to quality and quantity, but it is also essentially behaviouristic, i.e., the student is expected to *perform some kind of behaviour*. He is to tell, to define, to choose among, etc. The following examples of objectives may be judged by the reader to be well or badly described:

a Some ability to sing from notation.
b To be able at the age of nine to sing at sight whole tones and semitones, as well as repeated notes in the diatonic scale in a melody with crotchets and quavers in duple, triple, and quadruple time.
c A rather good knowledge of the staff notation when using tuned percussion instruments.
d To be able to play a sonata.
e To be able to play a sonata of a difficulty not exceeding that of, for instance, Mozart's *Sonata in C major*.
f To recognize, and name, different styles in piano music represented by pieces by composers such as Scarlatti, Mozart, Chopin, Debussy, Schönberg.

After having read a well defined objective one should be able to answer in detail, or with characteristic examples, what specific ability or knowledge is to be learnt and to what extent.

If an objective has been well defined it will be much easier to construct a progressive chain of steps in teaching, or more rightly, in creating opportunities for learning. In the modern sense of education a teacher does not really 'teach'. It is the pupil who learns. The teacher only creates opportunities for learning. Such a step-by-step procedure has become one of the characteristics of programmed instruction. Whether programmed or not it is, however—as we shall see in a following chapter—the hall-mark of all good instruction that it is well planned. To sum up then, first of all the planning of good instruction should start with a consideration of the sequence of psychological development in order to decide, from that point of view, what may be demanded at a specific age of the pupils. Secondly, the instructional objective should be well defined in terms of behaviour, i.e., the pupils should, after instruction, be able to perform something, or show a specified knowledge of something, to a certain specified extent. Thirdly, the special prerequisites of the subjects should be known or investigated. Fourthly, the instructional plan of learning should take form, and, if it is meant to become a detailed programmed instruction for general use, it should also be tested on several groups of the intended age, as well as younger and older ages, in order to produce a standardized version. The construction of a standardized tape-recorded programme, e.g., for learning and experiencing ear-training on musical intervals would, of necessity, take a considerable time to produce.

Educating Personality through Music

9

We have been occupied with the construction of educational objectives of music as a subject matter in the last chapter, but we must not forget that music education is not only concerned with the subject matter of music. It is also concerned with educating personality. The music teacher—if he works as a specialist—must not leave that aspect of education to his fellow-teachers. The education of personality is obviously the concern of all teachers. When school, for instance, demands of pupils that they sit at certain desks, that they are punctual, etc., this is establishing a feeling for order which a music teacher must cultivate as much as teachers in other subjects. Music as a school subject offers, however, certain possibilities of personality education which are peculiar to the subject and which may well be worth considering.

A lot of time in music periods is spent in listening to music. The main condition of learning through listening is the absence of boisterous noise. This is an uncompromising demand. The teacher must insist on the listener's *right to listen.* To disturb him by making a noise is to steal the listener's spiritual property. There is hardly any other school subject that makes such a definite demand for personal consideration. It is a demand which is made particularly upon less musical pupils, but for them to have to respect the right of their musical comrades to listen is a good training for personality. On the other hand a music teacher must not press the demand too far—which he does, if he selects music only for the talented children and neglects those who are not so musical. A realistic teacher must be fully aware that he will always have to compromise to some degree between artistry and what is possible from an educational point of view. A mutual consideration between teacher and pupils, their qualifications and interests, grows in a natural way with good teaching. The necessity for silence at times will then be respected.

Consideration for others is also a rule in an orchestra, choir, or smaller ensemble. Everyone cannot play the first violin or sing the solo. Those taking part must subordinate themselves in favour of the best possible performance as a whole.

But although he must subordinate himself in this way, taking part in musical instrumental or vocal groups usually *contributes to a pupil's self-respect*. Those who are not sufficiently proficient may be given other tasks, for instance, the organization of a group of listeners or the suggestion of a plan for a public performance. It is important that as many pupils as possible, whether more or less musical, are engaged in tasks of different kinds.

However, it is most natural for the musically able pupils to assert themselves through attempts at real musical achievements. A pupil who is known as a notorious nuisance may be given the task of conducting a school choir. If he puts up a good performance the success will not only affect his inclination to go on with music, it will probably positively affect even his manners on the whole, and his studies in subjects other than music. It is essential that musically gifted pupils be given the chance to assert themselves in music, lest they should assert themselves in other undesirable ways. There is something in the American idea of letting a brass-band accompany the football team of the school. In this way the musically gifted are given the same chance to assert themselves as the physically gifted.

The development of aesthetic taste is of course also within the scope of music education and a means of developing personality. It promotes interest in old and new culture, as well as tolerance towards different opinions of style and ethical norms. A civilized society should furnish its schools with sufficient resources for it to be able to encourage and develop the children's need for artistic expression and understanding of their national musical culture, past and present.

Musical culture is, however, not only of a national, but quite as much of an *international*, nature. Music education may, therefore, contribute to an international output of music. Artists from other countries, international musical terms, popular international melodies as well as internationally known serious works, awake a world-consciousness of other countries and their culture. To describe the music of foreign countries is a rewarding task for any music teacher and is a good means in creating local colour when teaching geography, or history of foreign countries.

That music education offers a solution to the *problem of spare time occupation* for many young people has been shown in a former chapter. In order to make a positive contribution in this respect the music teacher must, on the one hand, achieve really serious results in teaching the basic skills for making music, and, on the other, he must teach in such a way as to make his teaching popular, in the best sense of the word. A pupil who has acquired the skills of making music, and likes to make music, will probably have music as a good companion for the rest of his life.

School music should not isolate itself, but should co-operate with music teaching outside school. It should always seize opportunities of giving performances in connection with different school activities, such as exhibitions, church arrangements, or any other occasions of interest. Such performances help to arouse the interest of parents in music education and are of considerable importance for the pupil's self-respect.

What to Demand of a Good Teacher 10

In order to achieve the best results a teacher should satisfy certain demands. It may be convenient in the training of teachers to use a list of these demands when preparing lessons, and at the discussion and appraisal after teaching practice. There are, in this list, the important demands for Cognition, Clarity, and Contact, together with some Collateral demands (the four C's), and under these main headings we find some sub-headings. Each of these headings will be explained and dealt with in this chapter and, therefore, the list is also on the whole a disposition of the chapter. In addition to this disposition the chapter will include—as an instance of Clarity—some drafts of lessons under sub-headings that are not mentioned in the list. As a complement to the list a comparison with Fig. 26 will be convenient.

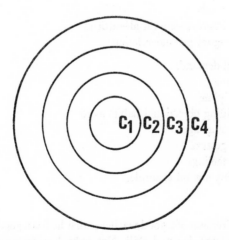

Fig. 26. C_1 (Cognition), C_2 (Clarity), C_3 (Contact), C_4 (Collateral demands), represented by a circle-diagram. The more central the more essential is a demand, i.e., a good cognition is essential for making good dispositions (clarity) and contact, but contact and clarity do not have much influence on cognition.

Demands

C$_1$ Cognition
C$_2$ Clarity
C$_3$ Contact *via*:
  1 the eye
  2 the ear
  3 the voice
  4 facial and bodily expressions
  5 questions and answers
  6 illustration
    a verbal
    b blackboard
    c other audio-visual aids
  7 personal interest and motivation
    a reward and punishment
    b halo effect
  8 attention factors (see chapter on Perception)
    a size
    b intensity
    c change and movement
    d repetition
    e needs
    f interest—appraisal—attitude
    g figure-ground-relation

C$_4$ Collateral demands
  1 Tempo
  2 Discipline
  3 Avoiding objectional habits as to
    a language
    b gesture
    c feelings
  4 Setting a good example.

Cognition

The first requirement of a good teacher is that he has a good professional cognition of knowledge and skill. Not only does an ignorant teacher run the risk of giving his pupils defective knowledge, but his own lack of knowledge or skill will also affect the clarity of his tuition and his appearance before his pupils, and make him uncertain and hesitant. Thus an imperfect cognition brings with it an imperfect clarity and contact. A class reacts with chatter and disorder. In individual instrumental tuition the pupil gets a feeling of uncertainty if, for instance, a tutor says a performance is not good but cannot himself show something better on the instrument, or otherwise clarify what he really means.

A good teacher prepares his lessons through control of his knowledge, which must come not only with the aid of the pupils' own textbooks, but also through reading professional papers and obtaining information of new methods and literature. In other words he must train and develop his own skill to set his pupils a good example.

Clarity

Clarity in teaching shows itself in the *disposition of the subject matter*. When preparing his lesson the teacher must plan the learning matter in sections and subsections and, if possible, also plan for the time available—allowing ten minutes for this, twenty minutes for that, and so on. Usually a lesson begins with a performance of the pupil's homework. This establishes a continuity between old and new learning matter. If homework has not been given the teacher should begin with some recapitulation of former subject matter instead. The new material is then to be submitted point by point according to the prepared disposition. Later we will see a few suggestions of such dispositions.

The music appreciation hour

An hour of music appreciation must not become an hour of listening at random to records chosen just to please the taste of the teacher or the pupils. The teacher should ask himself what he expects the pupils to learn through listening. In the lower grades it might be the difference between bass and treble, between *legato* and *staccato*, or different tempo markings. The teacher may choose for this purpose "Dance of the Elephants" from Saint-Saëns' *Carnival of the Animals*.[1] During his preparation the teacher has to decide what should come first: the name of the piece or the experience of the piece? He comes to the conclusion he had better start with the experience. That means he finds it most useful to play the record without mentioning the name either of the piece or of the composer. This will give him the opportunity of making the pupils themselves discover some characteristics that perhaps the title would have given away in advance. In order to guide the listening the teacher prepares some questions which may be distributed on a work-sheet to the pupils before listening. Thereafter, such a work-sheet becomes the disposition of the lesson. There may be questions like these:

[1] Columbia 33cx 1175. The record contains the whole *Carnival of the Animals* and, in addition, Britten's *A Young Person's Guide to the Orchestra*.

How do you want to name the piece?
□ "Song of the Lark"
□ "Elephants' Dance"
□ "Scent of Roses"

Which instrument plays the melody?
□ Double-bass
□ Flute
□ Piano

Are the notes of the melody mostly
□ High
□ Low?

Mark the answers you consider most correct.

When the piece has been played and the children have made their marks on the sheets, the teacher goes on to start a discussion about the music according to the plan he has prepared. This plan may correspond to a conversation like this:

—Why do you think the "Elephants' Dance" would be a suitable name for the piece?
—It sounded clumsy, so it could not be about larks or roses.
—Why do you think it sounded clumsy?
—The notes in the melody were low.
—Yes, they belonged to the bass, didn't they? How could you hear that it was a dance and not a 'song' or a 'scent'?

Rhythm and staccato come into the picture. The teacher's design for his lesson develops into something like the following:

A Five minutes of stimulating songs and voice training.

B "Dance of the Elephants" (main task: 30 minutes):

    1 Introduction and distribution of work-sheets

    2 Record played

    3 Answers to questions on work-sheet controlled by show of hands

    4 Conversation about questions and answers:
        a High and low, treble and bass (Why elephants?)
        b Staccato—legato (Why dance?)
        c Tempo (Why not a lullaby?)
        d Time (Did the animals waltz or twist?)
        e Short account of the composer and his country

5 Move like elephants to the music. The children stoop around in a ring, moving clumsily and clapping their hands behind their backs on the first beat of each measure. (The movement may be done in two ways. One way is to move one step to each beat. The other way is to move to the actual crotchets, quavers, and minims as they occur in the melody, i.e., one step to each note of the melody. Both ways may be used, calling the first way the "Old elephants way to dance", while the second way would be that of the elephant children. The pupils may be divided into two groups according to their ability to dance one way or the other.)

6 Percussion instruments are used to play a rhythm-*ostinato*, e.g., the first and last beat of each measure. (The *ostinato* may symbolize some other animal joining the dance.)

C   Five minutes of relaxing songs.

In the upper grades, of course, records and questions of a more advanced character are to be used. An example of this is shown later (page 122). Of course, a teacher would do better to have the disposition in his head rather than on paper, but to an inexperienced teacher it is good practice to write an outline on paper. Such an outline may also be useful and save time another year when the same lesson may be given to another class.

A singing lesson

The teaching of music appreciation may be rather similar to that of other subjects such as geography, history, or the arts. The *singing lesson*, however, is something quite different and must have its own disposition. A lesson solely made up of learning a song by imitating the teacher is, of course, not the objective, but some songs sometimes must be learned simply for the joy of singing. From other songs may be learned the elements of musical theory and sight singing, but let us first give some hints on how to learn songs without 'theory', using imagination rather than just imitation.

1 Play the tune once fast and once slowly. Ask what the text may be about in the different tempi. Reveal the correct tempo and content.

2 Read text in the rhythm of the tune.

3 Let the children sing the song on a syllable. In lower grades the syllable may symbolize some singing animal, or some pretended

foreign language. In higher grades it may be part of the deliberate voice training.

4 Play the tune and stop somewhere. Ask the children on what syllable in the text the break occurred.

5 Play the tune with a big mistake in pitch. Ask on what syllable in the text the fault was made. (The mistake must be big in order not to be confused with the correct note, causing an associative inhibition. This is not a pitch test!)

6 Play the tune with a big mistake in note-length. (See point 5.)

7 Underline accented syllables. Change the underlinings to bar-lines.

8a Count the phrases. Put a number where each phrase starts.

 b Play a phrase and ask which number was played.

 c Which phrases are similar and which dissimilar? Which are nearly alike, and what is the small difference in such a case?

9 Walk, run, or dance to the tune. One step to each beat.

10 Walk, run, or stand still exactly according to the rhythm of the song. One step to each note.

11 Dramatize the song with movements according to the contents.

12 Let boys and girls change places at the change of phrases.

13 Use percussion instruments.

 a Alter instrument at the change of phrases.

 b Use an *ostinato* rhythm throughout the tune.

14 Ask the children to draw an illustration to the song.

15 Text substitutions. Ask the children to suggest other animals, names, professions, etc., than the one originally mentioned in the text.

Some songs may be taught in this way in order to build a repertoire of songs and stimulate the children. Other songs must be used in such a way that notes and other elements of musical theory are learnt in an active way. A singing lesson should also include voice-training and in a modern singing lesson there are the great possibilities of using recorders, and tuned, as well as untuned percussion instruments too.

In the first grade when the children cannot read one must choose short songs with simple texts as, for instance, *Mary had a Little Lamb*. The teacher sings a phrase and asks: "What did I sing about?"— Mary. "What did she have as companion?"—A little lamb. "Would you like to have a lamb too?"—Yes. The teacher sings another phrase, talks about the phrase, makes the children repeat the phrase, both text and melody, draws a picture on the blackboard or puts up a picture of a lamb on a flannel board, dramatizes the song, uses untuned percussion instruments, etc. Eventually as the children learn to read and write, notes for use in simple *a vista* songs as well as simple tuned instruments are introduced. The children's animistic view of the environment should be used to the best advantage (see Chapter 7).

A singing lesson for pupils in the middle grades may be planned as follows.

A A well-known stimulating song. Voice training on some syllables.

B *The Ash Grove* to be learnt with the help of work-sheets (compare pp. 96–97), recorders, and percussion instruments.

    1 The teacher sings the song. Short note of the song's contents and origin.

    2 The teacher sings and plays with marked accents. The children underline accented syllables in the text.

    3 Underlinings are changed to bar lines.

    4 The time and time signature is stated. The children move their hands like conductors while listening to the melody. Eventually they sing on a syllable.

    5 The children listen to the song in too fast a tempo. The children discuss the tempo and decide that to suit the text it should be much calmer.

    6 The work-sheet is studied. There are some notes missing. The missing notes are filled in as a result of listening to and discussing the pitch, as well as measuring the notes.

    7 The text is read rhythmically and the song is sung.

    8 The class learns to clap the rhythm

    Counting numbers or reading syllables (taa taa saa taa taa saa, etc.), may be of help. When the clapping has gone on for a few bars, the teacher adds the melody to the *ostinato* rhythm. Take care that the children learn to clap softly. The rhythm may then be used on triangle or other suitable percussion instrument by a single pupil or a selected group, as shown in the arrangement on page 94. Since *The Ash Grove* provides an opportunity for teaching about the upbeat, the *ostinato* rhythm has been chosen to suit such an introduction.

    9 Same as point 8 with the exception that three children (or perhaps more than three) clap the rhythm on tambourines.

  10 The tambourine players play their rhythm. After two or four bars the rest of the class sing the song without clapping.

The Ash Grove

Arr. E. Franklin

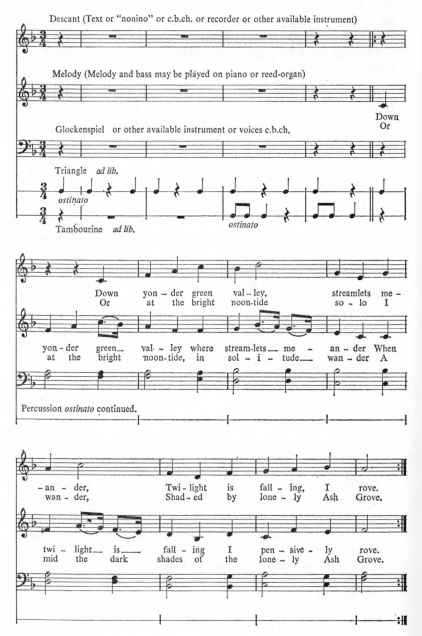

'Twas there while the blackbird was sin — ging its note, that I

'Twas there, while the blackbird was cheer-ful-ly sin-ging, I

Percussion *ostinato* continued.

met that dear one, the joy of my heart!

first met that dear one, the joy of my heart! A

A — round us for glad-ness, blue-bells were

round us for glad-ness the blue-bells were ring-ing; Ah!

ring-ing, litt — le I thought we should part.

then litt — le thought I how soon we should part.

11 Points 8, 9, and 10 are repeated with a new *ostinato* rhythm. This time a group of pupils use triangles with the rhythm

12 The song is sung with a prelude, i.e., the triangles start their *ostinato* four bars in advance, the tambourines two bars in advance.

13 A descant is learnt by able children with 'nono' (♩ ♩) and 'nonino' (♩. ♪ ♩), *or* with proposed text, *or* with recorder, *or* with Glockenspiel.

14 A bass may be added (but not necessarily) by the teacher or by children, if suitable instruments (cello, low Glockenspiels, guitar) are available, with skilled children.

15 Song and instruments are used to form a '*cantata*' with alternating solos and choir, instruments and descant. See page 94.

The kind of lesson produced is above all aimed at making music. When 'making' music, although so much is just learnt by heart and imitation, some notation and other musical theory is bound to be smuggled in. In order not to forget to establish a platform of musical theory it is advisable to use work-sheets as an aid. Eventually a collection of work-sheets is built up during the term and the teacher knows by going through his collection what has been done, or has still to be done, on the curriculum.

Work-sheet

The Ash Grove

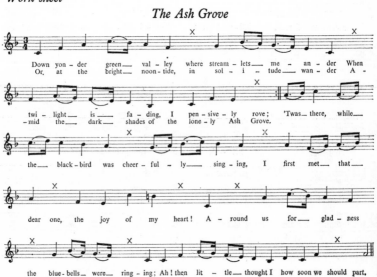

96

Exercise 1

Underline the most accented syllables of the text. Scan the text.

Exercise 2

Insert bar lines. The first bar line is to be written to the left of the word 'yonder'. The remaining bar lines are to be written to the left of each underlined syllable. Each staff need not necessarily end with a bar line.

Exercise 3

Which tempo (what speed) do you consider most suitable for the song? *Allegretto* (fast) or *Andante* (calmly)? Write whichever you consider to be the correct tempo to the left, above the uppermost lines of the notes.

Exercise 4

In some spots marked with a cross you will find a note missing. Try to find out through listening which will be the proper note and insert it first in pencil. Later you can use a ballpoint pen when your notes have been confirmed by your teacher.

Exercise 5

Here you will find a rhythm that you can learn to clap with your hands

or play on a percussion instrument: ♪ | ♪ ♩ ♪ | ♪ ♩ :‖

If you clap the rhythm to the tune of the song, such a rhythm is said to be *obligato*, because it serves as an accompaniment and has not got the same note-measures as the melody. If you do not make a break, but repeat this same rhythm as long as the melody lasts, the rhythm, in addition to *obligato*, will be called *ostinato*.

Exercise 6

Here is another rhythm that can be used *obligato* as well as *ostinato*:

♩ | ♫ ♪ ♩ | ♫ ♪ :‖

Text notation

Some music teachers may be hesitant about current methods of introducing notation in a singing class, since some methods are extremely tonal and build on the feeling for a tonic, while others are extremely atonal and build on the feeling for interval. Without claiming to be the herald of the only possible method I would like to point out the possibilities involved in using the song-text itself as a kind of notation. With this notation as a source we may, by way of substituting text-syllables for notes, introduce whatever musical styles, old or new, are possible in singing—together with terms and theory. As an example we may choose Béla Bartóks "Round Dance in Spring", adapted for our purpose from the composer's piano collection *For Children*. Our aim is to use the little song of 7 repeated bars to teach the children *a sharp*. If we want the children to get used to atonal song from the beginning of school, accidentals must be introduced at a very early stage. If we would rather use conventional music to start with, accidentals come at a later stage of tuition. The advantage of using text notation is that it may be used in both cases. Now let us see how it works.

Work-sheet

Round Dance in Spring

Béla Bartók

Transposed and adapted for text-notation by the author.[1]

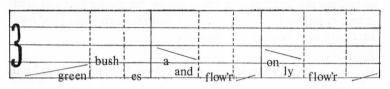

Complete what is missing in the staff translation.

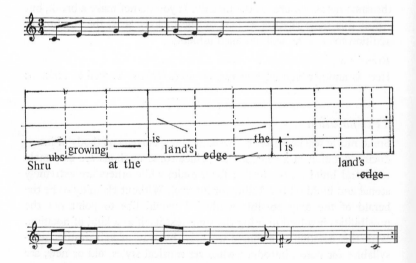

[1] The original piano piece is notated in the key of F major with *B flat* as the starting and final note. The note *E* is *flat* except in the sixth bar. The melody is a Slovakian folk tune.

The children get the song in this shape of notation. Having read the text and listened once or twice to the song performed by the teacher, they will be able to sing the song because they feel the pitch moving up and down with the text. This is of course the quintessence of the method: *to see the text on different levels of pitch forces the children to experience the coordination between seen level and sung level.*

The accidental sharp in the penultimate bar may be noted as an *arrow*. It may be there in advance and the teacher may ask the children: "Why that arrow?" It may, alternatively, be put in afterwards by the children as the result of a conversation on listening to the two bars preceding the last bar, containing the *F* as well as the *F sharp*. Thus the sharp is introduced in connection with actual music. The teacher may refer to the accidental as a deviation from the scale of the actual key, or he may call upon it as an indication of the intervals brought about. There is also an extension of note measures, an 'outwritten' *ritardando*, that goes together with the accidental. It brings about something definite and final in the expression, so the accidental sharp is not an 'accident' but a means of sharpening the expression.

As a final exercise the children may translate the whole song or part of the song into staff notation. In the actual work-sheet only a few bars have to be completed by the children. The areas within the dotted lines must, to begin with, have the same size. Eventually, as the children get used to text notation, the areas may be adapted to the text as in *Round Dance in Spring*.

Prerequisites for the translation of the whole song into staff notation are that the children have already learned:

1 the meaning of bar lines and dotted lines;
2 one text-crotchet gets one 'room' within dotted lines;
3 one staff-crotchet gets one beat;
4 text-quavers are overlined;
5 staff-quavers;
6 a text-minim is extended to another 'room' (beat) through a prolongation line;
7 staff-minims;
8 the short prolongation line of a dotted text-crotchet is overlined, indicating that the dot corresponds to a quaver;
9 dotted staff-crotchets;
10 names of lines, spaces, and ledgerlines of the staff notation.

This enumeration shows to some extent what may be learned eventually through text notation and translation into staff notation. Any song may be used to introduce one or the other element of musical theory, but the songs should be short, and the elements introduced, and practised, one at a time.

About the learning of the names of lines, spaces, and ledgers, it may be mentioned that they can be introduced in earlier translation exercises, in which case letters may be used instead of notes.

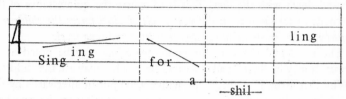

Text notation above, letter notes below.

It would be tempting to give examples of the introduction of each detail up to the consequent use of staff notation only, but I think it would be on the one hand pressing the method of text notation a little too far, and on the other guiding too much an imaginative teacher, who surely would rather choose songs and make work-sheets of his own. The final goal of music education is not to know the names of the notes but to be able to sing and make music with notes as a means of communication.

Activity with a pop-record

Songs recorded for the popular market may be used in music teaching. How many pupils were not already familiar with the songs of the Beatles when they were far down in the lower classes at school? How many teenagers did not find school music dull before their pop idols were allowed to be heard? It is entirely possible for 'pop' music to be used in music teaching but the activity connected with it must be something more than mere listening. The pupils must learn to use notes and terms and should not think that such knowledge is unnecessary in connection with this kind of music.

It may start very simply with the learning of crotchets and the corresponding rests. The pupils clap their hands on the notes and spread them on the rests in the following *ostinato* rhythms: ♩ ♩ ♩ ♩ :‖ and ♩ ♩ ♩ ♩ :‖. This they learn quite quickly. They also learn the terms quite rapidly, if they did not know them before. A pop record in ⁴⁄₄-time is then found to fit this rhythm. Instead of handclapping all kinds of untuned rhythm instruments can be used and variety introduced by dividing the class into groups, each group using one kind of instrument. The groups may then be instructed to play in different ways. One way is to change group and instrument at the beginning of each new phrase, sometimes using *tutti* as an emphatic effect at the end. Another way is to build dynamic terraces, i.e., start with one instrument on the first phrase, add another at the second phrase, still another at the third, and perhaps also the fourth, and then start afresh on the fifth phrase with only one instrument. Of course, it is also possible to take away one instrument at each new phrase. In fact there are still more possibilities for an inventive teacher. Let us see how it works with the refrain of Simon and Garfunkel's *Bye Bye, Love.*

The melody (chorus above, verse below) is excellent for training beginners on *recorders*. Only the notes used by the left hand need be learned. Of course, percussion can be used also with the verse in some way or another.

Bye Bye, Love

Felice Bryant and
Boudleaux Bryant

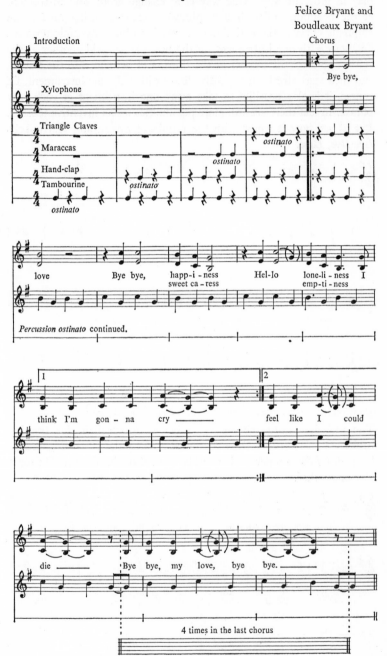

Verse

Recorder

There goes my ba – by   with some - one new ___
I'm through with ro - mance,   I'm through with love ___

Metalophone Alto

Tambourine

Other percussion *ostinato* as in chorus

___ She sure looks hap – py   I sure am blue ___
I'm through with coun – ting   the stars a - bove ___

___ She was my ba – by ___ till he stepped in ___
And here's the rea - son ___ that I'm so free ___

___ Good-bye to ro - mance ___ that might have been ___
My lo – vin' ba – by ___ is through with me ___

Pop records may be used for training with text notation.

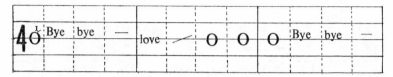

Text notation above. Staff notation below.

1⁄ O = nought (no notes) i.e., a rest

In higher classes a record may be given to an advanced group of pupils with the task of writing down the melody and text after simply listening to it, and then of adding an arrangement of their own with *ostinato* rhythms, melody fragments, and simple chords, for tuned and untuned rhythm instruments and also guitars, recorders, or whatever instruments they may be able to play in a simple way. The arrangement on pages 102–3 is the result of group work by student teachers at the conservatory of music in Gothenburg, who made the arrangement[1] as an accompaniment to the original record (CBS 63699), with some corrections by the author.

The method used may be briefly described as 'one thing at a time'. To begin with only one rhythm and instrument is combined with the record. If this is successful another *obligato* rhythm, or melody fragment, may be added, and so on. It is of course better to use a few instrumental groups with success than use a lot and have a débâcle. The pupils will probably realize that the volume of the record must be turned down in order to allow their own instruments to be heard. For instance, if violins are used *pizzicato* as tuned percussion, how are they to be heard at all if the records are played as loudly as possible? Thus the question of nuance, an important consideration in music appreciation, will arise.

[1] Reprinted by permission of Acuff-Rose Music Ltd. Special school arrangement from Simon and Garfunkel's record (CBS 63699) made by the author and a group of student teachers (text on pages 102–3), and intended for use in combination with the record. The music of the record *Bridge over Troubled Water* is also published for voice and piano. If this edition is used, together with the actual arrangement, it will have to be transposed from F to G major, and some small melodic changes will have to be made, corresponding to those made by Simon and Garfunkel.

Integration—groupwork—projects

Examples of lessons and methods have so far been rather limited. In the classroom situation the teacher is traditionally isolated with his class and his subject matter. In modern music teaching, as in other subjects, however, there is a movement towards breaking the isolation of one subject from other subjects through integration. At the same time there are attempts to end the isolation of the pupils from society by using current events and other matters of fact, especially those of interest to youth.

For a class teacher of the primary grades integration is most easily achieved, as she has the advantage of teaching all subjects herself. She may easily find suitable songs for use when teaching the children about different animals in natural history, or about different professions, or different countries and peoples, or different times of the year, such as Christmas, etc., for use in whatever is the subject for integration.

In the higher classes there is usually a different teacher for each subject, which means that there has to be contact between the teachers. A teacher of general history may get the idea of using Chopin's *Revolutionary Étude*[1] for creating colour in his teaching of the partition of Poland. A geography teacher preparing a lesson about the Far East may get the idea from the music teacher of using a record to create atmosphere for that subject.[2] Of course there should also be the same kind of co-operation between teachers of music and teachers of the history of arts. The real difficulty, however, arises if, for instance, one wants to co-ordinate the teaching of musical history with the teaching of general history, and history of the arts as well as of literature and religion, because such an arrangement would profoundly affect the curricula of all these subjects. Once achieved, the new over-all history curriculum would in turn have to be integrated with the curricula of other subjects such as geography and natural history. A beginning could be made with some limited over-all project where music would play a part together with other school subjects. For instance, France may be the subject of such a *project*, i.e., together with the study of France as a geographical subject goes the study of French history and constitution as well as French literature, art and music, contemporary and historical. The music teacher is one of a team of teachers who together plan the project which may well cover one or two months of teaching. This would not be difficult for a music teacher, as France

---

[1] Suggestions for records of Chopin's music are hardly necessary, as there are plenty of them on the market. Henceforth only some rather special records will be recommended. Although some of them will be deleted in time, they will serve as examples, and the music dealer will be able to suggest other suitable records of the same kind.

[2] e.g. *A Musical Anthology of the Orient* (Bärenreiter BM 30 L 2001-19).

has so much to offer in the field of music. The difficulty will probably not be co-ordination with other school subjects, but co-ordination with the special music curriculum, although with France as a project it could possibly be done. If the music curriculum says that the repertoire should include ten songs why not let a few of them be French? And if the curriculum says that dotted crotchets and semiquavers should be added to the notation knowledge, why not use French songs, eventually translated, if they contain the details necessary for this specific teaching? Examples of French music suitable in the teaching of music history will be even easier to find. For example Rameau's *Hen* and Saint-Saëns' *Carnival of the Animals* are ideal for young children, and Dukas' *The Sorcerer's Apprentice*, Debussy's *Claire de Lune*, and Ravel's *Danse Macabre* for rather older children. For pupils who are older still there is the whole repertoire from Lully up to modern composers like Messiaen. Thus the example of France as a project shows that the project method used in this integrative way offers a real possibility for the music teacher to break through the isolation that exists between his subject and other subjects at school.

The project method is usually combined with the practice of group work. This means that the teacher starts the project—or his part of the project when several teachers are co-working—with a lesson of stimulation. During this lesson he presents the subject as a whole and awakens the pupils' interest. The class is then divided into groups, and each group is given a special part of the subject to work on. This group work may take one hour or several hours, depending on the magnitude of the work. The different groups are finally brought together to show the teacher and each other the results. The teacher makes a summary, and sometimes also some kind of chart of acquired knowledge. So if the *Music of France* had been a project of music isolated from other school subjects, a group work would have started with a survey of French music. Different groups of pupils would then have started work on details such as French folk songs and folk music, French opera, French Impressionism, French music at the time of Purcell in England, contemporary French serious music, contemporary French popular music, songs from a French school song book, etc. This group work would have gone on for some time, and then the groups would have been brought together to show the results of their work. The results could have been shown in the form of short talks illustrated with music on record, or sung, or played on an instrument. The teacher would then have made a summary, and perhaps given the pupils some written questions. The conditions of such a group work is, of course, that there is a good music library of books and records available and also premises for reading and listening.

It should be mentioned that 'teaching in groups' is not the same as 'group work'. The teaching in groups is sometimes very useful in singing lessons. For instance, when learning a song, one group with a high average standard of achievement may become a group of descant singers. Another less able group may just accompany the song with a simple *ostinato* rhythm on untuned percussion instruments. A third group may use recorders, etc. Teaching in groups has also been used in teaching to play the recorder as well as teaching beginners on other different instruments.

Returning to the actual group work we will—after considering integration and group work as means of breaking the isolation between different school subjects—see if it can be used as a means of breaking the isolation between school music and society. Projects with this purpose must have an outlook on what is happening in society—what concerts are going on in the concert halls, what music there is on radio and television, what is the music of the season, what is the young people's music, what is serious as opposed to popular music? Such an outlook calls for projects like *Guitar music—old and modern, serious and popular, Avant-garde music, Origin and development of jazz, Popular tunes, Action music, Sound laboratories.*

A difficulty with the higher classes, where such projects as these are possible, is the difference in musical achievements between different pupils. Some have had training with instruments, others have not. Some have had really good music teaching by a class teacher, while some have just learned a few songs by heart. An advantage of using group work with a project is that the groups may be chosen so as to give pupils tasks corresponding to their ability in performance.

Let us see how a project like *Avant-garde music* may be worked out. It is meant to be used in the highest classes of a comprehensive school or a grammar school. The project may be limited to the actual avant-garde music of the street and the pop festival, but music education in school should have a wider aim and use the project for creation of *perspectives and tolerance of views and opinions.*

The project starts with a stimulation lesson. The teacher tries to *present the project* in such a way that it paves the way for a suitable division of the pupils into groups.

There are avant-gardes in all fields of human activity: religion, politics, economics, the arts, music, etc. Let us start with school music. If you considered yourself avant-gardists in school music what would you propose? Some of you may like to form a group in order to discuss school music. You could use the current official curriculum as one source. Other sources could be the public and school libraries. You could have interviews with school friends, teachers, musicians, and parents. In your report you could summarize your viewpoints, show songs you like and songs you dislike, etc. You should be prepared to discuss your viewpoints and give reasons. We may call this group the school music group.

The teacher continues with a presentation of the avant-garde within the context of serious music. There has always been an avant-garde within serious music, and within its framework we find great creators of new music and new musical movements through the ages. During the twentieth century some composers in the avant-garde have chosen to try and change the tone-system from the use of major and minor scales to the use of the chromatic scale in a twelve-note system. Thus the atonal music was created and later developed into serial music, so called in order to be distinguished from earlier tonal and thematic music. An instance of a twelve-note series is found in this book on page 21. Other examples may be found in libraries of books, note-sheets, and records. To begin with, the composers using the twelve-note system were very keen to use all the twelve notes of the chromatic scale in a series before being allowed to repeat a note. The following tasks may be of interest to a group working on atonalism.

1 How far can one proceed in any well-known song like, for example, *Greensleeves*, before any note is repeated?

2 Construct a twelve-note series in accordance with the rigid rule of twelve notes mentioned above. Try to develop it into a short composition.

3 How many times do you have to listen to a modern atonal work in order to get accustomed to it? For instance, take a movement from Blomdahl's symphony *Facets*[1] and compare it with a movement from a more conventional symphony by Sibelius or Nielsen.

4 Is the following melody tonal or atonal? Give reasons for your answer.[2]

5 Try to find out whether there exist series concerned with not only pitch but also strength and length of tones.

The report of the group can be given verbally with music illustrations.

[1] Discofil LT 33135, mono; SLT 33147, stereo.
[2] The twelve chromatic notes are used as a series. However, the notes E, G, and C are of considerable importance in suggesting a tonal chord. Perhaps it would be most correct to call the tune a compromise between tonality and atonality where apparently tonality has had the greatest influence.

The avant-garde composers did not only turn against the major and minor scales but also against the traditional musical instruments, whose means of expression were considered to be exhausted. Technological advances brought the new aids of tape recorders and electronic tone generators and thus the capability of creating any kinds of tones in successive and simultaneous combinations, i.e., the aids to produce *electronic music*. In addition the tape recorders provided means of using sounds other than those of musical instruments or electronic generators. Sounds of the surrounding world—even noisy ones—could be used in order to produce an organization of sound. Sounds from a garage, for instance, could be used together with the sounds of a bouncing ball. The human voice could be used, not for song or recitation, but as vowels and consonants, etc. This kind of music was called *musique concrète*. Electronic and concrete sounds may be mixed to what is called *electrophonic music*. These new musical movements demanded a new definition of music. Music was said to be 'organized sound'.[1]

To try and describe some opus in the genre, and also to produce some kind of tape music as a result of sound laboratory work, could be the task of a tape music group. The group must have a pair of tape recorders, an electronic tone producer, and some record of this kind of modern music. Simple producers of sine tones are often available in the physics departments of schools. Concrete sounds may be collected anywhere. Perhaps the result of the group work can be used as sound effects for some recitation or as a short overture of some dramatic school performance. *Aniara* is a good example of a modern opera work that may be mentioned as an example of a dramatic work using electronic effects.[2] One can also lower the demands of the tape music group and just allow the group to put sounds together at random. In this case the group is rather near to what is called *aleatoric music*. In this kind of music the composer prescribes that the performer improvises within certain rather wide limits, or that he chooses between certain alternatives provided by the composer. (See also footnote on page 37 as an instance.)

The tape music group will probably have great fun when producing their organization of sounds whatever it is. One thing that should also interest this group is the problem connected with the notation of modern music.

A fourth group may take up *action music* as their task. This kind of music has not much in common with conventional music but may rather be described as instrumental theatre. As a stimulating example

[1] Useful examples can be found on records: Philips AL 00565/66 (*International Music*) and Odeon PMCS 307 (*Swedish Music*).
[2] The Swedish composer Karl Birger Blomdahl for this opera has chosen a subject that tells the story of a spacecraft that gets lost in outer space.

the teacher may mention John Cage's *Water Music*, where the musician is instructed to pour water into a grand piano. In the piano there is a bowl, hidden from the listener-spectator. Karl-Erik Welin is one of the Swedish composers who have made experiments in this genre. The performance is often provocative and aims at making the listener-spectator strongly engaged in feeling sympathy or disapproval, anger, resentment, embarrassment, etc. Here is an example of La Monte Young. In one of his pieces he instructs the performer to push a piano towards a wall with the back of the piano against the wall. He must push as powerfully as possible. If the piano passes through the wall, he is instructed to go on pushing in the same direction, without any consideration of new obstacles, and continue to push as strongly as possible whether the piano is stopped by some obstacle or continues to roll. The piece is finished, when he is too exhausted to push any more.[1]

A group producing action music should have at least one member with explicit dramatic talent. The result depends a lot on the performers' dramatic and suggestive capacity. Some people consider action music to be just a sensation, while others take it seriously and expect a development.

The popular music has of course also developed. The vocalists have their microphones and guitars with electric amplifiers, as a result of technological advances. Electronic organs have also become popular instruments. There are also things happening to harmonization and other methods of arrangement in modern pop music which leave no doubt as to the existence of the avant-garde in the popular genre. It would be an interesting task to listen to pop records, old and new, and try to describe the real difference between them. Never satisfy yourself with phrases like "this is good" or "that is bad". Try to tell the difference in musical terms of instrumentation, form and harmony, improvisation, and the like. Part of the group, or a special group, could interest itself in jazz in order to map out what has been the development from the origin, and especially what is happening nowadays, in this kind of music.

The group (or groups) interested in pop music may have a look at the kind of activity with a pop record that is presented on pages 100–104. Perhaps that kind of occupation could suit the avant-garde group of popular music.

Thus the stimulation lesson or lessons are finished and the five groups, consisting of school music, twelve-note music, tape music, action music, and pop music, can be formed. The number of pupils in

---

[1] This example and further instances of action music are found in Jan Maegaard's *Musical Modernism*.

the class, the individual musical achievements, the access to different libraries and rooms, etc., are factors that affect the number of groups and the number of members in each group. It is also of great importance if the pupils have former experience of group work in other subjects than music, and from lower classes.

The instrumental lesson

The instrumental lesson is still another type of lesson. There are, of course, great differences on different levels and as to different instruments, or solo song. With beginners the lessons are somewhat pre-arranged, thanks to the learner's first book on the instrument. The tutor must not, however, spoon-feed a child with 'show and imitation'. If a child is shown a musical phrase ten times and imitates it ten times, he will probably learn the phrase. But one can hardly deny that demonstration on the part of the tutor may be evidence of lack of pedagogical imagination, just as it is a lack of imagination when a class teacher teaches a song repertoire through mere imitation.

An instrumental lesson practically always contains a performance of the pupil's homework. With beginners this part of the lesson should come first. With older pupils it is useful to start with some kind of warming up and flexing of muscles, training the touch on the keys of the piano, bowing on the violin, smoothing of the registers in voice training, etc. The rehearsal of homework often may continue with some suitable étude before the music piece is rehearsed. Then there is the new homework to be introduced to the pupil.

At the beginner stage the homework usually is just some page in the first piano (violin, clarinet, etc.) book. If the rehearsal turns out to be a good performance, one may go on to introduce another page of new homework. However, irrespective of whether the performance of homework is successful or not, the tutor should give the pupil some questions as a control.

—This was excellent, but why do you play as loudly as that?
—Because there is a *forte* in the notes.
—Right! And why do you play that black key instead of the white?
—Because that's how mother showed me. Isn't it right?
—Of course your mother was right, but how could she know? etc.

If one follows a certain outline the teacher will be able to recognize if the pupil has got assistance or not at home by the way of imitation instead of explanation. If one is content just to hear the pupil give a good performance, one knows nothing of how the result has been obtained and gaps in knowledge may escape observation and cause difficulties at a later stage.

When introducing notes, measures, etc., that are new to the child, it is advisable to follow up the example itself with more detailed tuition. When teaching new rhythms, it may be worthwhile making the pupil try the rhythm as an *ostinato* on a tambourine, while the tutor plays an improvised simple accompaniment on the piano. Beginners also derive much benefit from playing percussion instruments in groups. A tutor could well bring together the pupils in groups and not necessarily give all tuition individually. Piano pupils at even more advanced stages could learn a lot from, and find much pleasure in, playing together on tuned percussion instruments.

To sum up, it may be said that lessons with beginners should not be totally geared to the instrumental instruction book but should include other music, other ideas of method—such as Orff's *Music for Children* and the like—borrowed from methods of class teaching or from tuition of other instruments such as recorders, guitars, etc.

For an inexperienced teacher it may be well worthwhile using a list like the following and ticking off, as a control, what has been done at a lesson with beginners concerning the rehearsal of the homework, and also what has been regarded with reference to the new learning material.

A *Rehearsal of homework*
  1 Naming of notes
  2 Naming of measures
  3 Vocabulary of musical terms
  4 Practical performance as to
   a beat and rhythm
   b fingering
   c harmony, counterpoint
   d phrasing
   e feeling
   f position of hands and body, flexibility
   g pedals

B *Preparation of new lesson*
  1 Length and difficulty of new lesson
  2 What is new in the new piece, e.g., dotted quavers. How is this particular detail to be introduced and explained? Is the piano book clear enough on this point or must something else be added in order to clarify, or practise, the dotted note?
  3 Associative inhibitions to be prevented?
  4 How to arouse interest in the new piece?
  5 What to bring out in my own playing of the instrument?
  6 Applicable parts from details mentioned under *A* in the list.

An active tutor will eventually build up his own design for lessons suitable for beginners or more advanced pupils. The outline will of course differ from instrument to instrument. A tutor of the violin will have to insert points concerning bowing; a tutor of win dinstruments points about embouchure and breathing; a song tutor points on breathing, registers, and articulation.

In connection with the discussion of instrumental lessons what has been said about learning a piece of music in the chapter on the psychology of learning on page 69 should also be remembered.

Contact

The demand for contact, or communication, may be considered an overlapping demand. The cognizant teacher gets a better contact than the inexperienced, because the ignorant teacher will be uncertain in his approach. A well-planned lesson is a prerequisite for good contact, while a messy presentation of a subject brings about a breakdown of communication. Actually this is an overlapping from the inner circles (Fig. 26) to the outer. Possibly there may be some overlapping, but not so often, and not so easily proved, in the opposite direction. Because of a lack of communication the teacher may be confused about his own knowledge or skill and about his outline—but is he really deficient in any way? Does good contact give him any extra knowledge in his subject? The answer to this is probably not on lower levels of education but perhaps on the higher levels it does. He *may* alter the disposition of his lesson from one lesson to the other because of the results of good contact, i.e., suggestions and comments from the pupils revealing what otherwise would not have been known to the teacher.

The aspect of overlapping does not, however, interfere with our present view of separate means of contact at the teacher's disposal.

Contact of the eye

The contact of the eye is essential. The teacher fixes his eyes upon his pupils and also catches their eyes. In class teaching this is sometimes impossible if the instruments, pianos or reed-organs, are badly placed. Keyboard instruments should be located in such a way that the teacher is able to look at the children while accompanying songs. When teaching songs the teacher should, if possible, be unhindered by keyboard and notesheet, i.e., he should know the songs by heart and be able to improvise accompaniment of a simple character without losing his eye-contact with the class.

Eye-contact is especially important in choir and orchestral work. When performing a piece the conductor must have contact of the eyes from the very beginning to the last beat.

The individual piano tutor sits beside the piano and his pupil in order to be able to observe as much as possible. Although the tutor is sitting beside the pupil, they are both looking intently at note sheet and keyboard which thus act as intermediaries in maintaining eye-contact. If the tutor looks somewhere else, the pupil will immediately get the impression that the tutor's attention is slackening, and his performance will probably deteriorate.

Contact of the ear

The contact of the ear is obviously more important in music than in other school subjects. Music is the art of listening and producing for listening. At any musical performance the ear is the supreme authority: how did it sound; beautiful or ugly, strong or weak, soft or hard, personal or impersonal? For this reason you must not forget to listen continually and to teach your pupils to listen continually.

When performing individually on an instrument it is important that pupils are taught to *listen in advance*. If a note, or series of notes, have not been heard in advance, how can the pupil know whether he is playing loudly or quietly enough? In fact, pitch and strength and length of notes and chords should *not only be thought of in advance but thought in advance*! i.e., the inner musical ear of the brain should anticipate the perception, and control the muscle movements, in such a way that they will already be co-ordinated and when finally performed will correspond to the anticipation.

Of course it is of advantage for this purpose to train the pupils in sight singing. The class teachers who successfully train their children in sight singing are doing a service to the tutors of instruments and working for the benefit of the school choir.

Contact of the voice

Many people seem to be quite unconscious of the necessity of cultivating their voices, otherwise one would not hear so much weak and colourless speech. A teacher's voice must be strong enough to be heard by *all* pupils in a class, and also versatile enough to be raised or lowered when necessary for respect and attention.[1]

[1] A sound-level metre often reveals surprisingly big differences of sound level in different parts of a classroom and even within a short radius of the speaker. The importance of taking this into account, especially when using pure tones in a pitch test, has been pointed out by Desmond Sargent in a recent investigation. For connection between perception of pitch and loudness, see page 38.

A listener always experiences the voice as part of the speaker's personality. How will a teacher, using a very low, dreary, unemphatic voice be able to convey a lively interest in his subject to his pupils? Of course the voice has as much importance in individual tutoring. The voice of a teacher or tutor must be coloured by his personal interest in the subject matter, as shown by accents, pauses, rise and fall in speech melody, as well as by variations of strength. In the same way as an actor must moderate his voice in order to convey the correct impression of the part he is playing, so a music teacher must be a bit like an actor, and, if he is in the habit of using his voice without expression, he will have to train just like an actor to play his part in a class until he finds it natural to put interest and expression into his voice without 'acting'.

An interesting experiment may be done by anyone with a television set, alternatively using sound only or picture only. A comparison between sound and picture is overwhelming evidence of the necessity of voice as a means of expression, not only for what is said but how it is said. A music teacher must—besides expressing Debussy or any composer on his instrument—be able to interpret pictures and feelings and convince his pupils, that what he is conveying through his voice is important and interesting, whether he is telling a beginner that his minims sound like a clumsy bear or reproaching an advanced pupil with lack of feeling for the traits of Debussy's *The Girl with the Flaxen Hair*.

Facial and bodily expressions

In the same way as an actor, a music teacher may underline his words with facial expressions and gestures. These means of contact must not be overemphasized, but if they are used with moderation they may be of good service in underlining some important fact. A class teacher must not sit still at his desk, or at the instrument, all the time but move about in front of, and even sometimes among, the children in order to oversee what is going on among the pupils and in order to hold their attention.

For a tutor of solo song, facial expression and gestures are of more importance than to a class teacher, especially when using his influence on a pupil to put a voice in the right register, etc. The conductor of a choir or orchestra uses learned formalized gestures as well as improvised ones.

Questioning

A fundamental way to activate pupils is to ask questions. There are two different types: *heuristic* questions and *interrogative* questions.

Heuristic questions are of a leading type. They are used for introducing new learning matter in such a way that the pupils make discoveries and try to solve problems by themselves. Interrogative questions are used in order to check the children's homework or examine the pupils' knowledge.

According to an anecdote the principle of Archimedes was found accidentally on an occasion when Archimedes was taking his bath. He noticed that the water flowed over as he got into the bath and, realizing what it meant, exclaimed "Eureka!" (I have found it). He had discovered that a body, when sunk into a liquid, seemingly loses as much weight as the weight of the liquid that is pushed out of its place. Teaching becomes heuristic when it leads to new knowledge through the pupils' earlier experience. Let us take an example. The teacher is going to introduce Debussy and impressionism. He may start by playing the first movement of Beethoven's *Moonlight Sonata* and then immediately Debussy's *Claire de lune*. Then the field is open to heuristic questioning:

—Perhaps you know the pieces, but I will still ask you, which music do you think is the older?
—Why do you consider the first piece to be the older?
—In what way are the effects of the chords different in the second piece compared with the first?

From other angles one distinguishes between *determining* and *choosing* questions. An example of a determining question is: "Which music uses sine tones?" and of a choosing question: "Are sine tones used in concrete music or electronic music?" The determining question is the better of the two kinds. The choosing question provides the pupil with too great an opportunity to guess the correct answer. If the pupil is unable to answer one question, another question, differently formulated, may *lead* the pupil right. A leading question is often at the same time heuristic. A choosing question may sometimes serve as a leading question, but if a choosing question has been used it is advisable to let it be followed by a *why-question*.

—Is Schubert mainly romanticist or Viennese classicist?
—Romanticist.
—Why do you have that opinion?

A question may furthermore be either of a *longish* nature or be on *details*. In class teaching detail questions are usually preferred. A greater part of a class may be activated by short questions of detail rather than by lengthy ones. Besides it is easier to *spread* the questions among the children evenly. Pupils, who seldom or never get a question, find it unfair not to be attended to. Perhaps they very seldom put up their hands in order to get a question, but the chance will occur still more seldom if long questions are being used. However, long questions may be necessary if a pupil is to be given a chance to show knowledge and grasp in a wide context.

At individual tuition level the choice of question type will depend on time available and the achievements and skill of each pupil with reference to age and ability. Probably questioning could be used more than is usually the case in private tuition, especially questioning of the heuristic type.

Questioning must be *individualized* both in class teaching and individual tutoring to the extent of giving easy questions to a weak pupil and difficult questions to a pupil with greater ability.

Inexpedient questions are those of *filling in* and *repetition*. An example of filling in would be: "Of important interest to us in this connection is . . .? Anne." Anne is supposed to answer, for instance, "instrumentation". The shorter the pause between "is" and "Anne", the greater will be the possibility of misunderstanding. Perhaps Anne cannot answer at all, in which case she will become the object of interest herself instead of instrumentation. Sometimes this type of question becomes an awkward habit. The main reason, however, why filling in should not be used, is that the pupils fail to learn to make their own sentences.

Repetition of a question is inappropriate in that it seems to pre-suppose that the pupils are inattentive. If one feels that they have been attentive and heard the question it should not be necessary to repeat it. Instead a new question of the leading, heuristic type should be formulated.

Another viewpoint concerning questioning is that there should be a *pause* after the question has been asked in order to give the pupils time to think. Not until this pause has elapsed should the question be addressed to a certain pupil because if the choice is made before the question is asked only the pupil engaged in the question will be attentive, while the rest of the class will not care at all about the question.

If a pupil *cannot answer* a question correctly, he may be given a clue, or another pupil may take over the question, or—if time is short—the teacher may answer himself.

The *rhetorical* question—requiring no answer from the pupil because it is answered by the teacher himself—is a type that should not be used too often. It may, however, be advisable to use it if something has to be accentuated. For instance the teacher may raise a question like this: "The question we now have to answer is this: How did Wagner try to solve the conflict between musical and literary form? Let me answer.

He used what he called a *leading motive*, and we will see how it functioned."

In his teaching a teacher should use a polished colloquial English. Correct interrogatives should be used. Objectionable habits, such as an intervening 'er', should be eliminated.

Illustrative teaching

Illustrative teaching means that a point is made easy to understand through pictures and metaphors. For instance an orchestra may be compared with a football field—"Just as the ball is passed from one footballer to another, the musical theme passes from one instrument to another, from wind instruments to bowed instruments," etc.

The blackboard

Different audio-visual aids are used in illustrative teaching, the blackboard still being the most indispensable. In a room intended for music teaching the blackboard should have lines for staff notation. The spaces must not be too narrow, and in addition there must be room for ledger lines and song texts. Whatever is written must be easily legible from the seats farthest away. If the blackboard is to be used for different purposes the staff may be inserted on a transparency in an overhead projector (see also page 121). This is better than using a five-chalked tool, and drawing five lines at a time, because one rubs out lines as well as notes when correcting something or writing anything new. A duster does not take away the lines produced on the blackboard by an overhead projector.

When using the blackboard it is necessary to use the space to the best advantage. It is a good rule to start in the left-hand corner of the board. Names and terms are better remembered by the pupils if written on the board, because when they are repeated they are both heard and seen. Notices of this kind should not be written haphazardly but in a planned order. When speaking of a composer's life and work it may be convenient to use a time-line.

		Events	born 1770	French revolution 1789		etc.
Beethoven						
		Works		1804 *Eroica*		etc.

Sometimes an illustration rising in steps may be useful.

Beethoven (1770–1827)
Three periods

		1815–1827
	1803–1815	
1770–1803		

Another time it may be better to use columns.

Factors that had influence on Beethoven and his work

Nature	French revolution	Love	Deafness
Pastoral Symphony	*Fidelio*	*Sonata in C-sharp*	*5th Symphony*
Song of Praise	*Eroica*	*Für Elise*	*("Fate")*
etc.	*9th Symphony*	etc.	etc.
	etc.		

Theory of musical form will benefit from graphic representation; for instance, the introduction of a three part fugue:

	Subject (Comes)	Counter-subject
	————————	××××××××××
Subject (Dux)	Counter-subject	Continuance
————————	×××××××××× – – – – – – – – – – – – etc.	
		Subject (Dux)

Use of the graphic device of circles is demonstrated in Fig. 26, page 87. Divisions and subdivisions can be shown with lines or arrows:

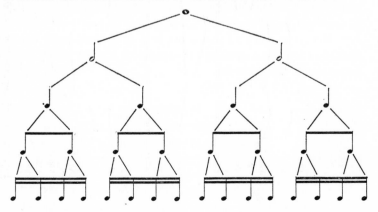

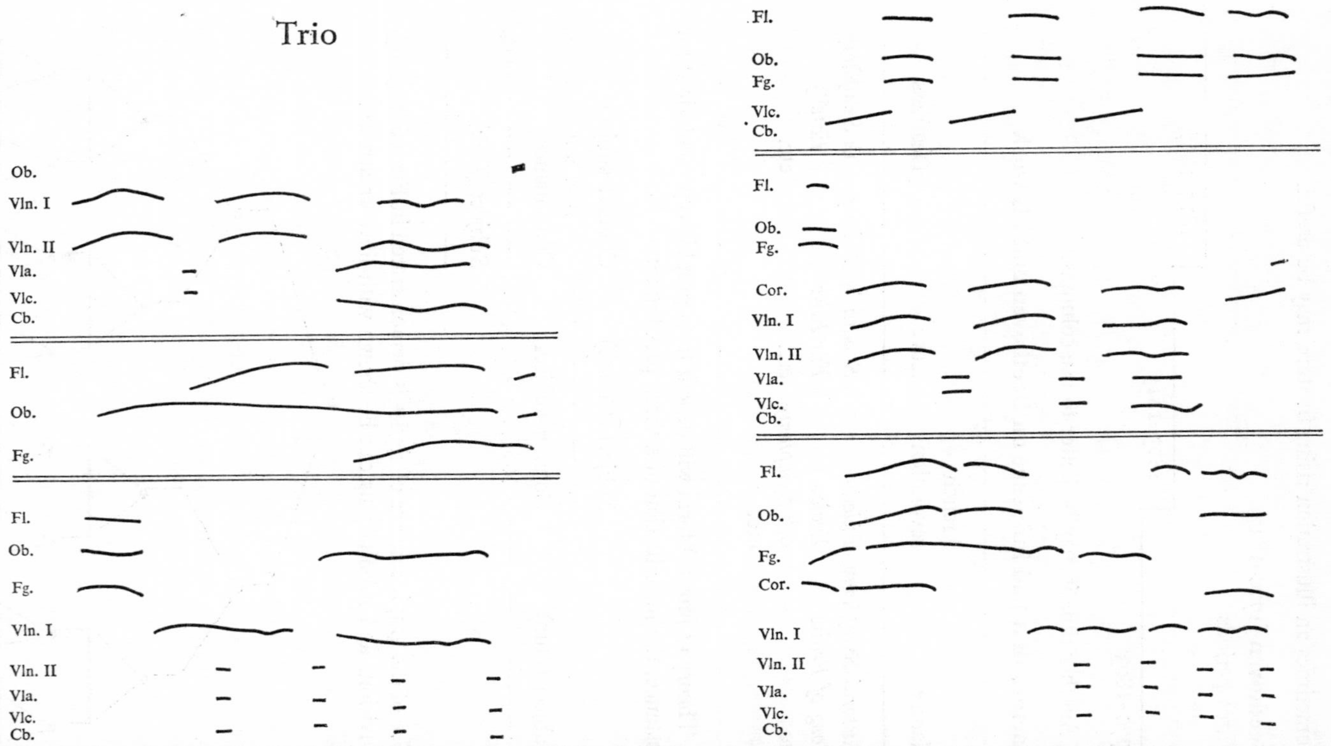

Trio

Fig. 27. Graphic representation of the instrumentation of the Trio from the third movement of Mozart's *Symphony No. 40 in G minor*. When translated on to a transparency each instrument should be represented by a different colour. This applies especially to the wind instruments.

Flannel board, magnet board, white board

Other aids are flannel and magnet board, as well as white board. The *flannel board* consists of a piece of flannel-covered board on which are fastened cut-out pieces. It may be used, for instance, to illustrate the introduction of the fugue, with six pieces of carton in four colours representing dux, comes, counter-subject, and continuance. Pupils may put the pieces on the board themselves. The fugue-exposition may be altered so as to start with an upper or a lower part, and in this case, a flannel board has an advantage over the blackboard, because the same pieces can be used for all the different alternatives and no duster has to be used. A *burdock board* is used in a similar way.

The *magnet board* is magnetic and implies that the pieces used for illustration are magnetized, i.e., made of steel or fastened to a piece of steel.

The *white board* consists of big leaves of white paper placed on a stand. The leaves may be turned like the pages of a book and an illustration thus grows step by step. The turning of the pages is accompanied by a verbal explanation.

The overhead projector

The material to work with in the overhead projector is the transparency. The teacher can draw or write in his own handwriting on the transparency or he can cut out illustrations from papers or books and have them photographed and transparencies made. It is always a good idea to have a copy of the work-sheet which is being distributed to the pupils, and, if possible, to prepare a transparency of it for the overhead projector or otherwise make copies of the exercises on the blackboard in order to be able to focus the attention and discuss the exercises with the students. It is convenient to have the music tape-recorded in order to get the advantage of being able to stop and repeat certain parts. In addition to the exercises on the work-sheet a teacher may of course improvise his own exercises and suggestions and discuss whatever he, or the pupils, may find interesting in the music observed. Certain notes may be left out in a theme and the pupils given the task of filling in what is missing. Alternatives of rhythms may be given and the pupils have the task of choosing which is correct, etc. An inventive teacher has a rich field for his imagination.

In addition to the work-sheets for lower forms presented earlier in this chapter, a work-sheet suitable for older pupils is given below. The music is Sæverud's *Rondo Amoroso, op. 14, no. 7.*[1] Besides being a

---

[1] The music is published separately for piano, and may easily be played by any music teacher. It is also available on record, His Master's Voice, ASCLP 1007. The title of the record is *Nordisk pianolyrik* (*Scandinavian Piano Lyrics*).

good instance of rondo form, this piece is also chosen for its interesting variations of style. The main rondo theme is easily recognizable as an old Viennese type, while the intervening themes are of a rather free and chromatic tonality.

A work-sheet of *this type is not intended for use as a kind of examination*. It is a series of listening exercises that the pupils themselves work through, *together with* the teacher. One exercise at a time is treated and each problem must be solved before proceeding to the next. Pupils should if possible be kept from looking ahead as the formulation of later questions may be an aid to solving problems in earlier questions.

Work-sheet

TO RECOGNIZE MUSICAL FORM

Within different arts we distinguish between form and content. For instance in literature we have novels, short stories, and poems. In music there are the forms of sonata, song, and rondo. The architectural frame in music, that settles the form as a whole, is often described by letters.

Sonata form	Exposition	Development	Recapitulation
	a b	Various treatment of *a* and *b*	*a b*

Three-part-song form　　*a   b   a* (the first *a* usually repeated)
Rondo form　　*a   b   a   c   .   .   .   a*

We see that repetition and contrast (see also page 19) are balanced in different ways in the different forms.

Exercise 1
Listen to a piece of music played by your teacher on the piano or a record. Is the piece in the form of a

a　☐　sonata
b　☐　three part song
c　☐　rondo

Tick which of the forms you consider correct.

Exercise 2
The piece contains five themes. Here are shown the notes beginning the themes. Which of the five themes is the real *rondo* subject? Mark below which you consider to be correct.

Exercise 3

Listen to the piece once more, and count how many times the main subject occurs. If you think that you observe the *rondo*-theme being played twice in succession it should be counted as twice.

Answer: The *rondo* theme occurs .... times.

Exercise 4

One of the other themes occurs as many as three times. Which is it? Put a mark before the theme you consider correct. (One theme is out of the running, if Exercise 2 is correctly answered. If this is the case, cross out the corresponding letter before this exercise is done.)

- ☐ A
- ☐ B
- ☐ C
- ☐ D
- ☐ E

Exercise 5

Listen to the piece once more. Try to mark with letters the themes in the order that they appear, just as if it were a conversation in a play. First Mr A speaks. Mr A is very talkative, so he repeats what he has already said. Miss B, however, has something to say too and eventually

Mrs C, etc. In this piece of conversation actually twelve contributions are made. So now consider yourself a secretary and make your record.
1...2...3...4...5...6...7...8...9...10...11...12....

Exercise 6
Which tempo do you think would be correct for this piece? Tick below whichever you consider correct.
☐ *Allegretto* (cheerful, not so quick as *allegro*)
☐ *Andante* ('easy-going' and rather slow)
☐ *Adagio* (very slow and expressive)

Exercise 7
As an introduction, we mentioned that a *rondo* consists of the parts *a b a c a . . . a*, where small letters were used in order to avoid confusion with the naming of the themes by capitals in the actual piece. Now try, with the aid of the result of Exercise 5, to bring together the capitals in groups in such a way that they suit the small letters of the rondo form:
      a ......
      b ......
      a ......
      c ......
      a ......

Exercise 8
What would you like to call this piece? There are reasons for either of two titles, but the composer has preferred one of them. Mark the name *you* would like to use.
      ☐ *Rondo Amoroso*
      ☐ *Rondo Allegretto*
      ☐ *Rondo Andante*

Exercise 9
Which composer would you suggest as having composed the piece? Mark who you think it was.
      ☐ Franz Joseph Haydn (1732–1809)
      ☐ Robert Schumann (1810–1856)
      ☐ Camille Saint-Saëns (1835–1921)
      ☐ Harald Sæverud (1897–   )

Exercise 10
Which sounds most modern, A or C? Tick the theme you consider the more modern.
      ☐ A
      ☐ C

Exercise	Correct answer
I	*c*
2	A
3	6 times
4	B
5	AA BCB AA DEB AA
6	*Allegretto*
7	*a* AA
	b BCB
	a AA
	c DEB
	a AA
8	Composer's title: *Rondo Amoroso*. Other acceptable title *Rondo Allegretto*. (*Amoroso* means lovingly, tenderly.)
9	Harald Sæverud
10	C

There are many rondos in classical literature to which the type of work-sheet presented above could be adapted, and among them are instances of the musical rondo form going hand in hand with the text in a song. A charming example of this is Herrick's *Cherry Ripe*, a very suitable song for an introduction to the rondo form. The work-sheet on page 96 (*The Ash Grove*) could easily be extended for such an introduction to the three-part-song form.

The aids that we have mentioned so far have been of a visual type. In music teaching the audio type is of special importance and we will now go on to this type of aid.

The tape recorder

The use of a tape recorder in conjunction with work-sheets has been mentioned previously. In addition film strips and overhead transparencies can also be used.

A school class may be taught rounds in such a way that they at first record the song in unison, and then sing it as a round with the recorder as one of the two parts.

When tutoring individually it is often of advantage to make a pupil listen to his own performance and, at the same time, check on the note sheet what needs more or less practice in order to be acceptable. A student in solo song may benefit from listening to his own voice, and experience it in the same way as other people do. To most people their own voice is a great surprise when they listen to it on a tape recorder for the first time.

Broadcast school programmes cannot always, or rather can very seldom, be used at all if they are not recorded, because the broadcasting programme seldom corresponds to the teacher's own timetable. Broadcast programmes are very useful if they are recorded and used at a time to suit the teacher's own schedule. Instruments used in the broadcast may have to be substituted for others in the teacher's own class. The radio commentator's advice and instructions usually have to be supplemented by those of the class teacher, etc. Often it is advisable to use the material of a radio lesson on two or three occasions in the teacher's own class, as the performance in a radio lesson rarely arises from just one lesson but is rather the result of several lessons with clever pupils. *Television* has not been used very much so far. It will, however, certainly be very useful as soon as videotape recorders can be had at a reasonable price for use in schools. *Films* of good quality for use in school music teaching so far have been rather few. The same is the case with *film-strips*. However, a teacher should follow the specialist press and snatch up what he may find useful. It is also valuable, of course, to attend courses, when new educational ideas are presented.

The singing note board

The singing note board may be used when training *a vista* song. When you use a special pointer, the spaces and lines 'sing' their pitch by means of an electronic system.

Personal interest

When going through different means of contact one must naturally also consider the teacher's *personal interest* in his pupils. Here one must again refer to Elisabeth Hurlock's well-known experiment (see page 58) in which the positive effect of *commendation* is evident. In its practical application, blame as well as credit must be used in order to suit the individual pupil. A weak pupil needs more praise than an able one. Getting one page in the piano book correct deserves credit for a weak pupil, but from a clever pupil one may demand three correct pages for the same amount of credit. Blame must also arise, but the pupil must not be corrected in such a way that he thinks the teacher has no confidence in him. If the teacher does not have confidence in him, how will he be able to have confidence in himself? If one deprives a pupil of his self-confidence, one has robbed him of his most valuable property. A failure must, of course, not be commended. The pupil will easily see through it, and the risk is that from then on he will not trust his teacher's opinion. But in connection with a failure a teacher may choose his words in such a way that they spur the pupil to start anew with fresh efforts. The worst thing to do is to ignore the pupil and not say a single word. The pupil has a right to know the result of his efforts.

It is of advantage if the teacher sometimes interests himself in things outside his musical province in case it would give a positive halo effect (word explanation on page 24). Obviously it must not encroach on the time intended for teaching, but there may be, for instance, occasionally an opportunity at the beginning or at the end of lessons. A little talk about what may interest the pupils may result in an improved contact.

Attention

Attention is, of course, very important in teaching. It is, however, fully dealt with in connection with perception and attention from the psychological point of view. As the methodological aspects of attention are very apparent, and striking applications of the psychological aspects have already been dealt with (see page 22), it is clearly of little use to repeat them in this chapter.

Order

Questions of order and discipline need not arise in individual tutoring. When using group methods, or general class teaching, such problems may arise, and it is necessary to pay some attention to them.

There are two main causes of disciplinary problems, bad teaching and the verticality of the class as a group.

Importance of teaching ability

The most devastating cause of bad order is *bad teaching*—inability to rouse interest, dead pauses, teaching beyond the pupils' level of apprehension, etc.

The class as a vertical group

The second main cause of difficulties with discipline is that the teacher has to keep together, in one class, *pupils of differing degrees of talent, weak as well as clever*. In this respect a class is 'vertical'. Pupils, who are hardly able to keep to the tune when singing, are taught together with class mates who are able to sing *a vista* without difficulty. To keep order under these circumstances is not always so easy. Pupils of low intelligence are often placed in special classes, and as a consequence an ordinary class with reference to general subjects is a little more horizontal. This does not help the music teacher, however, because musical talent does not go together with general talent. A solution of the problem may be to divide a class into *horizontal groups* as regards musical achievement, i.e., pupils of the same musical standard are placed together in each group. Such a grouping is advisable when a teacher eventually creates different opportunities for activity in his class. One may work with groups of singers, recorders, percussion instruments (tuned and untuned), or readers, listening and writing (music history or theory). When the class is together as a whole, the teacher will, of course, mainly be interested in the average standard of the class. However, it will be necessary for him to show interest not only in the highly but also in the less highly talented children, and not neglect to choose examples for them to listen to and songs for them to add to their repertoire, etc.

Disciplinary measures

If the order is imperfect in a class something must be done about it. The *placing* of pupils may be changed. The desks may be arranged semi-circularly instead of in straight rows. They may, perhaps, be placed nearer to the teacher and his instrument, or the teacher and his instrument may be moved nearer to the children. The children may stand and form a group round the teacher and his instrument. An especially troublesome pupil may be moved from one desk to another. He may be placed right in front of the teacher, or at the very back of the room.

Just to *look* at a disturbing child—without interrupting the teaching —may sometimes be enough. It should certainly be the first thing to try with an inattentive pupil. Disturbing pupils mostly do not like being observed and so stop chattering. To *give a question* to an inattentive child or his friend beside him is often effective. It has the same advantage as the method of using the eyes, because the teacher can keep his teaching going at the same time. The question used should, of course, be one that was going to be given to the class anyway. Sometimes a very *short break* in the teacher's speech together with an observant eye on the pupil may be needed. If these steps prove ineffective a break in the teaching may be necessary for a *reprimand* to be given. The next step—if repeated rebuke is ineffective—should be a *private talk* with the noisy one. This private talk must aim at getting to know the real underlying cause of the nuisance. Quite often the reason is a feeling of inferiority. The pupil is inferior in music. He tries to compensate for his feeling of inferiority by drawing attention to himself in other ways. Such a problem is one that often arises out of the cause already mentioned as 'the class as a vertical group' and the remedy may be a horizontal grouping of the class, or the entrusting of the individual pupil with some special task. Knowledge of the pupil's background and contact with the home are always desirable.

If the music teacher does not succeed in getting to know the underlying cause he should *ask his colleagues* whether they have the same trouble and whether there may be some common reason for disturbance if it happens in other subjects too. The *principal of the school* should be consulted. Proceedings like *ordering out of the classroom* should not be used at first, and only resorted to very seldom. Even more drastic steps, like *expulsion* from school, must be preceded by a very thorough investigation of the case, in which the music teacher must take part with the others. The music teacher should not underestimate his role in such an investigation, because the music lessons, and also individual instrumental lessons, may offer some special insight into the problem.

The teacher setting an example

In his appearance a teacher should set an example to his pupils. He should keep his temper, and control his gestures and feelings. A teacher who loses his temper will quickly lose the respect of his class. He will probably at the same time lose his own self-respect. His self-respect, as well as the respect of others, will grow with devoted and loyal work, careful preparation of his lessons, and so on.

The Music Teacher and School Democracy

In the discussion about order and discipline we have hitherto covered practical matters and given some advice. The problems concerning order and discipline should, however, also be dealt with in a wider context, against the background of the development of society and socio-psychological research. In the practical educational debate this has been summarized in the concept of school democracy.

Democracy is a Greek word meaning 'rule by the people'. School democracy should therefore imply 'rule by the people at school'.

Different levels of age and maturity call for correspondingly different levels of the meaning of democracy. School democracy may be looked upon as a demand from society that school should educate the children to be mature for the democracy of adult society. This education for democracy functions at school in such a way that the pupils gradually, as they grow in age and maturity, take more and more responsibility in the school society. Simultaneously the role of the teacher becomes gradually less determining and more advising.

Contributions of social psychology

Among contributions from social psychology to the debate of school democracy we find the development of sociometric methods and experiments concerning different types of leadership.

A sociometric experiment in a class may be done as follows. The teacher asks each of his pupils to write on a paper the names of three friends that he would like to have with him during a sports day, during a group work, during an excursion, etc. The result is first put in a tabular form and then transformed into a sociogram. There are different sorts of sociogram but a usual form is circular and looks like a target with concentric circles. Near the centre is the most popular child, while in the periphery we find the recluses. The relationships between pupils are shown with arrows, and with the help of these it is possible to discover sets within the class.

These sociometric methods are of great value in socio-psychologic research, but their use in practical school work must not be over-emphasized. Perhaps it may be useful when starting something voluntarily, a choir for instance. Of course one wants to have the most

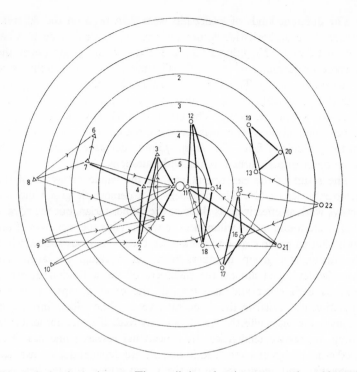

Fig. 28. A circular sociogram. The pupils in a class (average age about 8½ years) have answered the question which three friends they want to be with during an excursion. Thin lines are choices in one direction only. Double lines are mutual choices. The sociogram shows that girls (rings), and boys (triangles), form two separate groups. In the centre we find one girl and one boy. They are both chosen by five class mates. In the periphery are the boys, numbered 8, 9, and 10, as well as the girl numbered 22. They are evidently not so popular. In the group of girls we find three sets. Some of the children have only chosen two friends. The pupil numbered 6 was absent.

musical pupils in the choir, but it may be useful to know not only if they are musical, but also how they get on with one another. For instance, if a pupil may be either a soprano or an alto then the voice is no basis for decision, but the evidence of the sociogram may point to placing the pupil in the same section of the choir as his special school-mate.

Democratically speaking sociometric methods may be considered a kind of voting by ballot.

The Americans Lippitt and White, in 1939, performed an experiment on leadership, in which they used boys of eleven who were divided into groups, each busy with a hobby activity. Some youth leaders were engaged and trained to execute roles as authoritarian, democratic, or *laissez-faire* leaders.

The different kinds of leadership were then tried on the different groups. The authoritarian leader determined himself in detail what was to be done. No information was given to the group about the purpose or planning of the work. The members of the group were criticized personally. The democratic leader planned the work together with the group and suggested different ways of proceeding which were discussed within the group. The group as a whole decided what was to be done and how. The members were not criticized personally but on the grounds of facts. The *laissez-faire* leader gave instruction only when the members turned to him with questions.

The result of the experiment was on the whole in favour of the democratic leadership. The members of a democratic group did not always work as effectively as those of the authoritarian, but the advantages were found in the willingness to work. Thus the members of the authoritarian group ceased to work when their leader was absent, while the democratic group members went on working. An aggressive attitude developed among the members of the authoritarian group towards each other and also towards the other groups, while co-operation was usual in the democratic group. The *laissez-faire* group attained the least effective result and showed, like the authoritarian group, aggressive tendencies. In educational research one has often used other designations than authoritarian and democratic, for instance, *dominative* and *integrative* respectively concerning the teacher as a leader of the work at school.

In voluntary work with study circles in music, choirs, and amateur orchestras, the experiment is literally applicable. That the planning is done mutually between the leader and the members is essential when choosing notes, records, books, and other learning material, as well as when making the outline of studies and practice. From this common planning there is created, from the very beginning, a common interest and an aim at fulfilling the undertaking.

The significance of the experiment with reference to the school class is that the personal attitude of a teacher towards the pupils is shown to be very important. Above all the teacher must convince his pupils of a sincere wish to co-operate. The pupils are not only to be provided with tasks and exercises to perform and solve themselves, but must get a feeling that the teacher is willing to share the difficulties with them and do his best in order to help them. Democracy at school is experienced on a fundamental level in the immediate contact between teacher and pupils in the class room. Let us see how it can show itself in a lesson in one of the higher classes at a comprehensive school or a grammar school.

The teacher intends to speak about musical form and has chosen as an illustration the second movement of Haydn's *Symphony No.* 94 *in G major* (see Fig. 2, page 14). One of the students is opposed to learning 'only' about classical music at school. The teacher brings the question up for discussion. This discussion results in comparisons between the Haydn movement and a pop tune. Both kinds of music are listened to in order to find similarities and dissimilarities. A fundamental similarity as to the harmonious ground pillars (tonic, dominant, subdominant) is found. Also they are found to have the two fundamental form-creative principles of repetition and contrast in common. The difference consists in what is developed out of the musical idea: a minuet, a waltz, a pop-tune, or a whole symphonic movement. The conversation between the teacher and his pupils has led to a fruitful result, which may be quite a good foundation on which to build a wider knowledge of musical form.

In the instance of Haydn and the pop tune one should observe the importance of keeping order during a discussion. In order to maintain this order it is necessary to use the democratic principle of *freedom of speech*. An educational discussion must not degenerate into a common murmur, where the strongest voice will have the most weighty influence. Education for democracy must imply that the pupils learn to put up their hands and ask for permission to speak. It is about the same thing that happens when an MP asks permission to speak and is given the floor. There is, however, a difference between the old school and the modern in that when a pupil raised his hand in the old school it could only mean that he considered himself able to answer his master's question. In the modern school it means in addition, that the pupil may want to ask his teacher a question, or tell his school friends something, or start a discussion. The custom of raising your hand is indeed a good democratic arrangement, and, besides, it is a quiet custom. The teacher acts as a chairman. At some discussions it may be convenient for the pupils to elect one of themselves as chairman.

All teaching cannot be arranged in this way, however. For instance, when using methods of individualized programmed instruction it is quite impossible. The teacher is also bound by curricula and timetables, so it is a question of time and effectiveness. As has been said before, it is also necessary to take the maturity of the children of different levels into consideration.

Levels of management, decision, and contact

Different school systems have their rules and customs concerning pupils participating in school committees and staff meetings. It is a good arrangement in order to train pupils for democracy, and also for the benefit of a good contact between staff, teachers, and pupils. The music teacher usually has a very good contact through his orchestral and choir work, as well as in teaching both classes and individuals in instrumental music. However, this should not prevent a music teacher from making use of other means of contact within the framework of school democracy, e.g., work on committees and boards, not only for the benefit of contact as such, but also for the benefit of music as a subject.

Literature

It is obviously quite impossible to give a complete list of works covering the wide field of psychological and educational specialities dealt with in this book. The following bibliography therefore—with few exceptions—is limited to some introductory and comprehensive works, from which the reader can obtain further information. Special sources for this book have been the author's Thesis on Tonality and the *Journal of Research in Music Education* both mentioned below.

General Psychology and Education

Anastasi, A. *Psychological Testing*, Macmillan 1968
Baldwin, A. L. *Theories of Child Development*, Wiley 1967
Bany, M. A. & Johnston, L. V. *Classroom Group Behaviour*, New York: Macmillan, London: Collier-Macmillan 1964
Bruner, J. S. *The Process of Education*, Harvard University Press 1960
Fernald, L. D. & Fernald, P. S. *Overview of General Psychology*, Boston: Houghton Mifflin, London: Harrap 1966
Gage, N. L., ed. *Handbook of Research on Teaching*, Rand-McNally 1963
Gagné, R. M. *The Conditions of Learning*, Holt, Rinehart and Winston 1965
Garrett, H. E. *Great Experiments in Psychology*, Appleton-Century-Crofts 1951
Gesell, A. & Ilg, F. L. *The Child from Five to Ten*, Hamish Hamilton 1946
Green, D. R. *Educational Psychology*, Prentice-Hall 1964
Jackson, S. *A Teacher's Guide to Tests*, Longman 1968
Maddox, H. *How to Study*, Pan 1963
Manuel, H. T. *Elementary Statistics for Teachers*, American Book Co. 1962
Maxwell, J. *Pupil and Teacher. An Introduction to Educational Pyschology*, Harrap 1969
Mednick, S. A. *Learning*, Prentice-Hall 1964
Montagnon, F. & Bennet, R. *What is Programmed Learning?* BBC Publications 1965
Pinsent, A. *The Principles of Teaching Method*, Harrap 3rd rev. ed. 1969
Sandström, C. L. *The Psychology of Childhood and Adolescence*, Methuen 1966

Music Psychology and Education

Benade, A. *Horns, Strings and Harmony*, Educational Services, Watertown, Mass. 1960
Bentley, A. *Musical Ability in Children and Its Measurement*, Harrap 1966
Bergeijk, W. A. van & Pierce, J. R. & David, Jr E. E. *Waves and the Ear*, Educational Services, Watertown, Mass. 1960

Brocklehurst, B. *Response to Music*, Routledge & Kegan Paul 1971

Colwell, R. *The Evaluation of Music Teaching and Learning*, Prentice-Hall 1970

Council for Research in Music Education (Bulletins published regularly, no. 21 Summer 1970), Ed. office: Colwell & Kusk, 57 E. Armory, Champaign, Illinois

Farnsworth, P. R. *The Social Psychology of Music*, Dryden, New York 1958

Franklin, E. *Tonality as a Basis for the Study of Musical Talent*, Akademiförlaget, Gothenburg. Contains the author's individual Tonality Test.

Grant, W. *Music in Education*, Proc. 14th symposium of the Colston Research Society, Butterworth 1963

Holmström, L.-G. *Musicality and Prognosis*, Almqvist and Wiksells, Uppsala 1963

Journal of Research in Music Education, Vol. XVII, no. 1 (1969). Papers of the International Seminar on Experimental Research in Music Education, Reading, England, 1968. Washington D.C.: Music Educators National Conference. The journal contains 28 articles representative of the present state of music educational research.

Kurth, E. *Musikpsychologie*, Krompholz, Bern 1947

Langley, E. *Principles of Teaching as Applied to Music*, London 1963

Lehman, P. R. *Tests and Measurements in Music*, Prentice-Hall 1968

Lundin, R. W. *An Objective Psychology of Music*, Ronald 1967

Mursell, J. L. *The Psychology of Music*, Norton 1937

Mursell, J. L. *Education for Musical Growth*, Ginn 1948

Mursell, J. L. & Glenn, M. *The Psychology of School Music Teaching*, Silver Burdett, New York 1931

Rainbow, B. *Handbook for Music Teachers*, Methuen 2nd ed. 1968

Révész, G. *Introduction to the Psychology of Music*, Longman (Eng. translation) 1953

Schoen, M. *The Psychology of Music*, Roland Press 1940

Seashore, C. E. *Psychology of Music*, McGraw-Hill 1938

Shuter, R. *The Psychology of Musical Ability*, Methuen 1968

Music Tests

The tests mentioned below are those described in Chapter 5 and are in the same order as in that chapter. An extensive description of published tests is available in Chapter 8 of Colwell's *The Evaluation*, etc. (see bibliography above). See also Lehman's *Tests and Measurements*, etc. (also mentioned above).

Seashore: *Measures of Musical Talent*, Seashore, C. & Lewis, D., & Saetveit, J., The Psychological Corporation, New York, rev. ed. 1960

Wing: *Standardized Tests of Musical Intelligence*, National Foundation for Educational Research, The Mere, Upton Park, Slough, Bucks., England. The test battery is described in *Tests of Musical Ability and Appreciation*, Cambridge University Press 2nd ed. 1968. The battery is also called *The Wing Musical Aptitude Test*.

Holmström: The Holmström battery is published in Swedish only. See, however, the constructor's above-mentioned thesis (1963).

Bentley: *Measures of Musical Abilities*, Harrap. See the constructor's above mentioned book (1966).

Gordon: *Musical Aptitude Profile*, Houghton Mifflin 1965

Franklin: *Individual TMT-test*, published in thesis mentioned above (1956).

Colwell: *Music Achievement Tests*, Follett Educational Corporation, Chicago, Illinois 1968–70

Kwalwasser & Dykema: *K-D Music Tests*, Carl Fisher, New York 1930

Drake: *Drake Musical Aptitude Tests*, Science Research Association, Chicago, Illinois, 2nd ed. 1957

Whistler & Thorpe: *Musical Aptitude Test*, Test Bureau, Los Angeles, Calif. 1950

Index